W9-CUB-729

MAKE YOUR OWN
CUSHIONS & COVERS

*For Michael, Michelle,
Nina and Nicolaas*

MAKE YOUR OWN CUSHIONS & COVERS

LANI VAN REENEN

PHOTOGRAPHS BY JUAN ESPI
ILLUSTRATIONS BY JANE FENEMORE

A Storey Publishing Book

STOREY

Storey Communications, Inc.
Schoolhouse Road
Pownal, Vermont 05261

United States edition published in 1994 by Storey Communications, Inc., Schoolhouse Road, Pownal, Vermont 05261.
United Kingdom edition published in 1993 by New Holland (Publishers) Ltd., 37 Connaught Street, London W2 2AZ.

Storey Communications, Inc. editor: Deborah Balmuth
Editors: Sandie Vahl and Elizabeth Frost
Designers: Janice Evans and Lellyn Creamer
Photographer: Juan Espi
Illustrator: Jane Fenemore
Photographic stylist: Elaine Levitte

Typesetting by Diatype Setting CC
Reproduction by Unifoto (Pty) Ltd.
Printed and bound in Singapore by Kyodo Printing Co (Pte) Ltd.

TITLE PAGE: A variation of the rose pin-tuck and lace quilt using green prints and plain cream. Ruched over-cloths with bows over plain round table-cloths decorate the drape tables, and scatter cushions with frills and decorative fronts complete the picture.

RIGHT: Two dainty bolster-style neck cushions decorated with border prints and frills.

Library of Congress Cataloging-in-Publication Data
Van Reenen, Lani.
Make your own cushions & covers / Lani van Reenen; photographs by Juan Espi; illustrations by Jane Fenemore.

Includes bibliographical references and index.
ISBN 0-88266-875-7: $18.95
1. Cushions. 2. Coverlets. 3. Tablecloths. I. Title.
II. Title: Make your own cushions and covers.
TT387.V36 1994
646.2—dc20   94-1411
CIP

ACKNOWLEDGEMENTS
The publishers would like to thank Pru Pfuhl and the Biggie Best chain of interior decorating shops for their invaluable help in creating this book.

CONTENTS

INTRODUCTION

Making soft furnishings affords us the opportunity to personalise and individualise our surroundings. Through the creative and innovative use of fabrics, we can introduce an element of 'softness' to our homes, and, as a bonus, enjoy the tremendous sense of achievement and pleasure we derive from applying our creativity in this way. To me, this is the essence of home decorating.

As my ideas for *Cushions & Covers* took shape, it became clear that I would have to build myself some framework within which to develop this concept. 'Cushions' was pretty straightforward; for 'Covers', I decided to limit myself to those covers we use in a bedroom – and, because this book is all about using fabric in imaginative ways, I decided to extend my definition of covers to include hangings around four-poster beds and other interesting ideas such as mock four-posters and corona drapes.

I have attempted to keep the instructions basic and easy to follow, but have assumed that you have a fundamental knowledge of sewing techniques. Often the items described in the text have been embellished with decorative finishes for the photographs; I hope these will inspire and encourage you to be similarly adventurous.

It was not possible to be too directive about sizes of items or quantities of fabrics for bolsters or covers for the bedroom because of the versatility of bolsters and the variety of bedroom furniture that exists. It is therefore important that accurate measurements are taken and the relevant formulas are used to determine the amount of fabric required for each item you wish to make.

Modern concepts and styles of decorating draw on home furnishings ideas across the ages. Fabrics in natural earthy cotton are now widely available in many designs, which range from casual to classic, romantic to restrained, understated to boldly dramatic, and in a wide selection of colour themes. There is endless scope for co-ordination and the opportunity for individuality. Many ranges, which include borders and lace, are also complemented by wallpaper, bed linen, decorative china, and decorating accessories such as lampshades, mirrors, pictures, coatracks and many small gift items.

In this book, I have divulged many professional secrets, for those of you who look at quilts and cushions in the shops and think, 'I'm sure I can make that myself'. There are also some brand new ideas that follow the latest trends in decorating. Whatever you choose to make, I sincerely hope that you experience the pleasure of stepping back and saying, 'I made that!'

OPPOSITE: A corona over a bed, a cream dream quilt, ribbon and lace trimming on a gathered nightfrill and a scatter of lace cushions create a bedroom out of another era.

OVERLEAF: These flat-bordered cushions, with their crisp neat lines, and tailored piped cushions in paisley are for those who dislike frills and flounces.

PART ONE

CUSHIONS

To me, the word cushion is synonymous with comfort. Other associations that come to mind are cosiness, informality, relaxation and homeliness. I think these associations are common to most of us and that the image of a sofa or bed piled with cushions is a pleasing and satisfying one both emotionally and aesthetically. Scatter cushions, bolsters and boxed cushions are therefore an important decorating tool in creating a warm and welcoming atmosphere, be it in the lounge, bedroom, dining-room, kitchen or outdoors. They also serve to transform hard, uncomfortable chairs and benches or areas such as bay windows, wide window-sills or a bricked-up recess in a wall into comfortable extra seating space. Adding cushions to a decorating scheme also creates the opportunity to introduce contrasts and accents and visually to tie the whole look of a room together. For a bold and dramatic touch introduce a new colour or fabric design to create a focal point; or, for a subtle, understated and co-ordinated look, repeat the colour and designs used elsewhere in the room, for instance, in tie-backs, valances, borders, table-cloths, swags and tails. The style of the cushions should be in harmony with the decorative style of the rest of the room. A formal lounge may be softened by the introduction of scatter cushions, but these should be more formal, such as plain or piped cushions, or cushions with flat borders. A feminine atmosphere in a bedroom could be enhanced by the introduction of cushions with frills and pin-tucks or lace and ribbon trimmings. The colour and fabric designs of the cushions should be 'sympathetic' to the background against which they will be displayed and should make decorating 'sense'. So, if you plan to introduce a few colour accents and different fabric designs by means of scatter cushions, ensure that there is some common link between them. Have some matching pairs amongst the collection of cushions and arrange them casually to create a relaxed atmosphere.

SCATTER CUSHIONS

There is a great variety of cushion shapes: square, rectangular, round and even fun shapes like hearts and cats. In the right setting, a combination of shapes and sizes may go down well, but, generally, I would suggest that you keep to the more practical and versatile square, rectangular or round shapes.

Materials for inner pads

You may have existing inner pads needing new covers or you can buy ready made pads. However, inner pads are easy to make out of calico, lining, ticking, sheets or left-over fabric.
  The following types of stuffing or fillings are available:

Foam chips (shredded foam) This is the cheapest filling, but it needs to be packed firmly and evenly to prevent the finished cushion from looking lumpy. This filling is ideal for cushions that will be used in children's rooms, for big floor cushions and cushions to be used outdoors.

Polyester wadding (batting) Sold by the metre (yard). This is relatively cheap and completely washable, and is most suitable for quilts. Also available as polyester fibrefill for making pads for scatter cushions.

Polyester granules (styrofoam pellets) These small beads are mainly used to fill large floor cushions or 'bean bags'. The granules move about inside the cushion to accommodate the sitter.

Feathers and down These are luxurious and expensive fillings. They naturally plump up cushions and give them a more sophisticated look and feel. A mixture of down and feathers costs slightly less than 100 per cent down and it creates the right balance between plumpness and lightness. Special downproof material should be used for the inner pad, and a double row of small stitches for seams will prevent any of the stuffing from working its way out.

Solid foam pieces Low- or high-density foam pieces are ideal for cushions that need a definite shape and firmness, such as cushions for dining-room chairs, a bay window seat or other hard surfaces.

Making inner pads

A good size for a scatter cushion is from 35 cm (14 in) square to 40 cm (16 in) square and 35 cm to 40 cm (14 in to 16 in) diameter for a round cushion (excluding frills). Calculate the size of the inner pad accordingly.

> **HINT** *Inner pads should be 1 cm (⅜ in) larger than the finished size of the cushion for a plump effect and good fit.*

REQUIREMENTS
Fabric: calico, lining, ticking or left-overs
Filling of your choice

METHOD FOR A SQUARE OR ROUND INNER PAD
1. *Cut out two pieces of fabric for inner pad to required size. Remember to add on a 1 cm (⅜ in) seam allowance all round. (See p. 11 for pattern.)*
2. *With right sides together, sew along three sides. On the fourth side, sew in about 10 cm (4 in) on each side, leaving an opening to get your hand through (about 15 cm [6 in]).*
3. *Clip corners for a square inner pad; notch seam allowance for a round inner pad. Turn right side out, and poke out corners. Press.*
4. *Stuff inner pad firmly with filling of your choice, and slip-stitch opening closed.*

Making a pattern for cushion covers

You can transfer your measurements for the cushion cover (see below) directly onto the fabric, but it is better to make a paper pattern. The advantages of using a paper pattern are that you can centre your pattern more carefully onto a large floral design, and it saves you time if you are going to make quite a few cushions of the same size.

❏ For a *square or rectangular cushion cover*, measure the width and length of the inner pad, seam to seam. For a plump, snug fit, which is preferable for most scatter cushions, do not add any seam allowance.

❏ For a *round cushion cover*, measure the diameter of the inner pad, seam to seam. For a snug fit, do not allow any seam allowance. Cut a square of paper slightly larger than this measurement, and fold it in half and then in half again. Tie a piece of string to a pencil, and push the other end of the string into the corner of the folded paper, with a drawing pin, at exactly the distance of the radius (diameter ÷ 2) from the pencil point. Draw a quarter circle *(Fig. 1)*. Cut out the pattern on this line through all thicknesses.

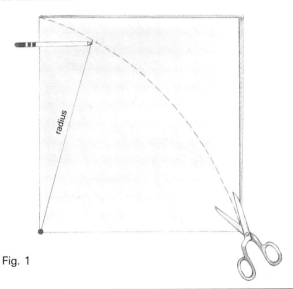

radius

Fig. 1

Zips and openings

Because not all inner pads are washable, it is important that cushion covers can be removed easily when they need to be washed. Any of the following openings can be used for cushion covers:

Zip in the seam

The advantage of having a zip opening in the seam is that the front and the back of the cushion are equally attractive.

METHOD FOR A SQUARE CUSHION COVER

1. *Cut two squares of fabric according to pattern for a square cushion cover (see opposite), and position them with right sides together.*

2. *Sew in from each corner on one side, leaving a central opening for zip (the zip should measure three-quarters of the length of the side seam). Tack opening along seam line, and press seam open (Fig. 2a).*

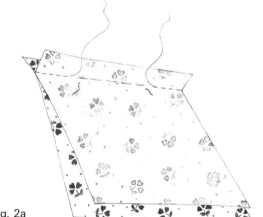

Fig. 2a

3. *Position zip face-down, centrally, over tacked part of the seam on wrong side of the fabric, and tack it into position* (Fig. 2b).

Fig. 2b

4. *Stitch all round zip with zip foot. Undo tacking, and open zip.*

5. *With right sides together, sew round remaining three sides of cover. Clip corners, turn cover right side out, and press (Fig. 2c).*

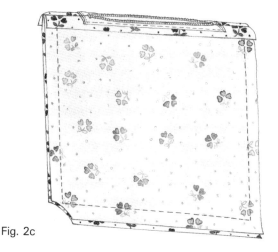

Fig. 2c

Zip across the back

METHOD FOR A SQUARE CUSHION COVER

1. *Add 3 cm (1¼ in) to the width of your pattern for the cushion cover back (p. 11), and cut out resulting rectangle of fabric. Cut this rectangle in half. (See also Fig. 6a, p. 13.)*

2. *Align two cut edges with right sides together, and sew in from two corners (seam allowance is 1.5 cm [⅝ in]), leaving an opening for zip (the zip should measure three-quarters of the width of the cushion). Tack opening along seam line, and press seam open. (Fig. 3a.)*

3. *Sew in zip (steps 3 and 4, pp. 11–12; Fig. 3b).*

Fig. 3a

Fig. 3b

COMPLETING THE COVER *When you have made your back opening (zip across the back, pp. 12–13; overlap opening, pp. 13–14; or buttons across the back, p. 14), you should have a square or round piece the size of your pattern piece (p. 11). With right sides and raw edges together, position back on front (zip or buttons open!), and sew all round the cover. Clip corners (square cover) or notch seam allowance (round cover), turn right side out, and press (Fig. 4a; Fig. 4b).*

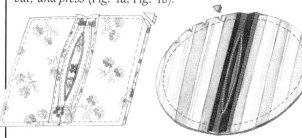

Fig. 4a

Fig. 4b

METHOD FOR A ROUND CUSHION COVER

1. *Cut through centre of your pattern for a round cushion cover for the back* (p. 11).

2. *Position resulting two pieces of pattern on fabric, leaving a 3 cm (1¼ in) space between them, and draw a line along centre of this space (Fig. 5a). Cut along this line and round the pattern pieces.*

3. *With right sides of cut edges together, sew 1.5 cm (⅝ in) seams at both ends, leaving an opening for the zip about three-quarters the diameter of cushion (Fig. 5b). Tack opening along seam line, and press open.*

4. *Sew in zip (steps 3 and 4, pp. 11–12).*

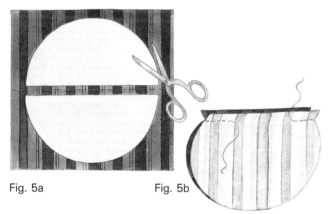

Fig. 5a   Fig. 5b

Overlap opening

This type of back opening is often used for small scatter cushions. It is neat, provides easy access to the inner pad, and is by far the easiest to make.

METHOD FOR A SQUARE CUSHION COVER

1. *There should be an overlap of 10 cm (4 in) at the back. Thus, add 12 cm (4¾ in) to the width of your pattern for the cushion cover back (Fig. 6a), and cut out the resulting rectangle of fabric.*

2. *Cut rectangle of fabric in half widthwise (Fig. 6a).*

3. *Finish cut edges by overlocking or zigzagging them, and stitching down a 1 cm (⅜ in) hem on the two edges that will overlap (Fig. 6b).*

4. *Overlap the two pieces of fabric by 10 cm (4 in) to match the original pattern (p. 11), and sew overlap down on each side (Fig. 6c).*

12 cm (4¾ in)

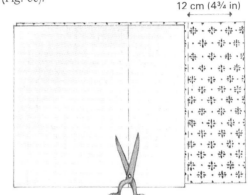

Fig. 6a

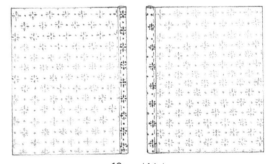

Fig. 6b

10 cm (4 in)

Fig. 6c

METHOD FOR A ROUND CUSHION COVER

1. *Proceed exactly as for a square cushion cover* (steps 1–4, p. 13), *using the diameter as a measurement.*
2. *Position paper pattern for a round cushion cover* (p. 11) *on top of the resulting square, and cut out round the pattern* (Fig. 7).

Fig. 8

Fig. 7

METHOD FOR A ROUND CUSHION COVER

1. *Proceed exactly as for square cushion cover* (steps 1–4), *using the diameter of the cushion as the measurement.*
2. *Position pattern for a round cushion cover on the square, and cut out round the pattern* (Fig. 9).

Fig. 9

Buttons across the back

METHOD FOR A SQUARE CUSHION COVER

1. *Add 5 cm (2 in) to width of your pattern for the cushion cover back* (p. 11), *and cut out resulting rectangle of fabric. Cut this rectangle in half widthwise* (Fig. 6a, p. 13).
2. *Overlock or zigzag cut edges, and fold over a 2 cm (¾ in) hem to the wrong sides of fabric. Stitch close to overlocked edges* (Fig. 8).
3. *Position hem of one side over hem of other side, pin and mark positions for buttons and buttonholes* (Fig. 8).
4. *Separate, make buttonholes, and sew on buttons. Fasten buttons, and tack ends together.*

Side openings with bows

Instead of concealing the cushion cover opening, make it a feature by tying contrasting bands of fabric into bows along a side opening.

HINT *This type of opening can be used effectively on regular-sized and continental pillowcases. Position the bows on one end of the pillowcase only.*

MEASURING

Add a 1.5 cm (⅝ in) seam allowance to inner pad measurement all round *(p. 10)*. Cut out a paper pattern (A) for back and front cover *(p. 11)*. Cut out a rectangular pattern (B) for the inside pocket flap using the length of pattern A and a width of 15 cm (6 in). Cut out pattern C for binding using the length measurement of pattern A and a width of 5 cm (2 in). (See below for ties.)

REQUIREMENTS
Paper pattern: A, B and C
Fabric: 2 × A, 2 × B, 2 × C
Contrast fabric for ties: 8 pieces, each 25 cm × 5 cm (10 in × 2 in)
Inner pad

METHOD
1. *Use pattern A to cut out two pieces of fabric for back and front; use pattern B to cut out two pieces of fabric for inside pocket flap; use pattern C to cut out two pieces of fabric for binding.*
2. *Make ties by folding in and sewing down a very narrow double hem on two long and one short side of each fabric strip. Press seams.*
3. *With right sides and raw edges together, pin two ties at equal distances along the width side of the cushion cover front and back.*
4. *Sew a 5 mm (¼ in) hem along one long side of one inside pocket flap (B). With right sides and raw edges together, position pocket flap over cushion cover front (with ties attached in step 3) and sew a 1.5 cm (⅝ in) seam across (Fig. 10a). Repeat steps 3 and 4 for other side.*
5. *With right sides and raw edges together, position one binding piece (C) over the cushion cover back (with ties attached in step 3) and sew a 1.5 cm (⅝ in) seam across (Fig. 10b). Press in a 5 mm (¼ in) hem on the raw edge of binding, turn over to the wrong side, and sew it down. Do the same on the other side, and press (Fig. 10c).*

6. *With right sides and raw edges together, position front cover on back cover, and sew 1.5 cm (⅝ in) side seams (Fig. 10d). Insert inner pad under the two pocket flaps, and tie the bands into bows.*

> **HINT** *Piping can be sewn round the cushion front before the ties are pinned into position in step 3.*

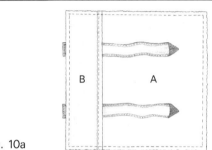

Fig. 10a

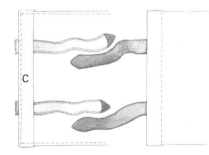

Fig. 10b

Fig. 10c

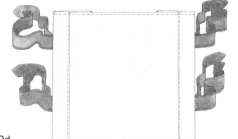

Fig. 10d

Piped cushions

These neat cushions, in square or round shapes, can be used in most decorating schemes. They are a good choice on a sofa with elegant, formal proportions, but happily blend with a variety of other styles. They look good in plain colours with matching or contrasting piping. Experiment with piping in a floral or striped fabric, repeating fabrics used elsewhere in the room. You can also make a feature of the piping by using an extra thick piping cord – about the thickness of a pencil. The size of the cushions should be proportional to the furniture, bench or window-sill on which they will be displayed and to the other cushions being used.

REQUIREMENTS
Paper pattern (p. 11)
Fabric for front and back (p. 18)
Piping: enough to go round cushion plus a bit
extra for joining (p. 18)
Inner pad

METHOD FOR A SQUARE OR ROUND CUSHION COVER
1. *Cut out cushion cover front, using pattern.*
2. *Decide on back opening, and proceed according to instructions* (pp. 12–14).
3. *Tack piping to right side of the front, keeping raw edges of piping and fabric together (the piping should meet in the centre of one of the sides). Clip into piping seam allowance at corners for square cushion cover* (Fig. 11a). *For round cushion cover, clip into piping seam allowance at regular intervals* (Fig. 11b). *Stitch on the piping along seam line using the zip foot.*
4. *Join ends of the piping neatly* (p. 66).
5. *With right sides and raw edges together, position back of the cushion cover (zip or buttons open!) over front, and tack and stitch on previous stitching line* (step 3) *using the zip foot.*

6. *Clip corners (square cushion cover) or notch the seam allowance (round cushion cover), turn right side out, and press. Insert inner pad.*

Fig. 11a

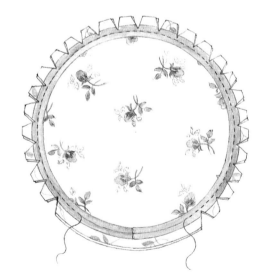

Fig. 11b

Piped cushion with gathered corners (square)

The same method as for a piped square cushion is used. The corners of the front and back pieces are folded into gathers, pinned, and basted before the piping is attached *(Fig. 12)*. This gives the cushion an almost three-dimensional appearance, which is ideal for larger seating or back-rest cushions. The inner pad for this cushion must be firmly stuffed.

Fig. 12

Piped cushion with a frill

This is probably the most popular style for scatter cushions and ideal when using a range of co-ordinating fabrics. The style is easy and relaxed, pretty and feminine, and will soften even the most severe surroundings. The opportunities to introduce fabrics of contrasting colour and design to subtly co-ordinate with the total decorating scheme of a room are endless.

A popular size for these cushions is from 35 cm (14 in) to 40 cm (16 in) for a square cushion and 35 cm to 40 cm (14 in to 16 in) diameter for a round cushion, with a 5 cm to 7 cm (2 in to 3 in) frill.

REQUIREMENTS
Paper pattern (p. 11)
Fabric for front and back (p. 18)
Fabric for frill (p. 18)
Piping: enough to go round cushion plus a bit extra for joining (p. 18)
Inner pad

METHOD
1. *Cut out cushion cover front using paper pattern.*
2. *Cut and make up back of cushion cover according to back opening you choose (pp. 12–14).*
3. *Cut out strips for frill, and join them by means of French seams (step 6, p. 42) to form a circle (Fig. 13a).*
4. *Press and stitch a narrow double hem on raw edge of one side of strip.*
5. *Divide circle into quarters, and mark or pin it on wrong side of remaining raw edge. Sew zigzag stitching over a strong thread, like crochet cotton (Fig. 13b), along this raw edge right round. (Do not gather at this stage.)*
6. *Tack piping to right side of cushion cover front, with raw edges together (piping should meet in centre of one of the sides). Clip into seam allowance of piping at corners for*

Fig. 13a

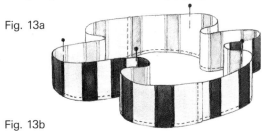

Fig. 13b

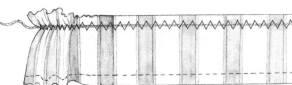

17

square cushion cover. For round cushion cover, clip into piping seam allowance at regular intervals. (Fig. 11a and Fig. 11b, p. 16.) Join ends of piping neatly (p. 66).

7. Pin the four marks on the ungathered frill to four corners of cushion cover front (or for round cushion cover, to marks made at regular intervals), and draw in cotton threads to gather frill equally to fit each side or round the cover. Pin and tack frill down. (Fig. 13c; Fig. 13d.)

8. Finally, pin and tack cushion cover back over the front, right sides and raw edges together (zip or buttons open), and stitch right round cover using zip foot. Sew as close to piping as possible. (Fig. 13e.)

9. Trim seams, unpick tacking stitches and gathering threads, and turn right side out. Press. Insert inner pad.

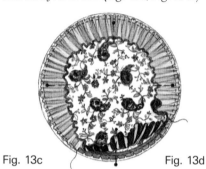

Fig. 13c

Fig. 13d

Fig. 13e

TYPE OF CUSHION	SIZE	FABRIC FOR COVER*	FABRIC FOR FRILL, CONTRAST OR TIES (width = 150 cm [60 in])	PIPING	BINDING	LACE
Piped	Square: 35 cm (14 in) Round: 35 cm (14 in) diameter	38 cm (15 in)		Square: 1.45 m (57 in) Round: 1.15 m (45 in)		
Piped and frilled	Square: 35 cm (14 in) Round: 35 cm (14 in) diameter	38 cm (15 in)	Single frill: 20 cm (8 in) Double frill: 32 cm (12½ in) Contrast back: 20 cm (8 in) Edging front: 15 cm (6 in)	Square: 1.45 m (57 in) Round: 1.15 m (45 in)	Square: 3 m (3¼ yd) Round: 2.4 m (2¾ yd)	Square: 3 m (3¼ yd) Round: 2.3 m (2¾ yd)
Single flat border	35 cm (14 in) sq	50 cm (20 in)				
Double flat border	35 cm (14 in) sq with 5 cm (2 in) border	65 cm (26 in)				
Double flat contrasting border	35 cm (14 in) sq	50 cm (20 in)	50 cm (20 in)			
Contrast border 'frame' made of mitred strips	35 cm (14 in) sq with 6 cm (2¼ in) border	50 cm (20 in)	36 cm (14½ in)			
Side opening with bows	35 cm (14 in) sq	38 cm (15 in)	15 cm (6 in)	1.45 m (57 in)		

*Add on for type of opening you use

Alternative ideas for frills and edgings

❏ Add *lace edging* to a single frill.

❏ *Gather two single frills,* with the front frill narrower than the back. A lace edging on the front frill shows off beautifully against the wider back frill. Alternatively, the front fabric frill can be replaced with a broad lace frill.

❏ *Contrasting binding* in a plain or patterned fabric looks lovely on the edge of a frill and makes it stand out crisply. Use ready-made binding or cut your own *(p. 65),* using the measurement of the length of the ungathered frill. Sew it onto one of the raw edges of the frill before gathering *(step 7, p. 18).*

❏ A *double frill* is made with a double thickness of fabric. It must be used on all reversible items such as duvet covers. Double the width required for the finished size of the frill and add a 3 cm (1¼ in) seam allowance. Cut strips, join them, fold in half lengthwise, and press and gather the raw edge *(Fig. 13b, p. 17).*

❏ A variation of a double frill is a *contrasting back frill edging the front frill.* To make this frill:

1. *Cut strips for back frill 3 cm (1¼ in) wider than front frill. Join strips so that you have one continuous strip for the front frill and one for the back frill.*

2. *With right sides together, join back frill to front frill* (Fig. 14a) *along the length of one raw edge.*

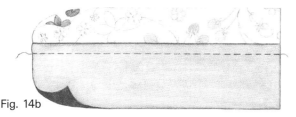

Fig. 14a

3. *Press seam towards shorter front frill* (Fig. 14b).

Fig. 14b

4. *Position raw edges of the wrong sides together, and press flat. The wider back strip will fold over to show in front* (Fig. 14c).

Fig. 14c

❏ Broderie anglaise lace in varying widths in traditional cream and white as well as in other pastel shades and patterns can be lovely when used as frills, especially on scatter cushions and pillowcases in the bedroom.

❏ *Border fabrics* are very attractive when they are used as frills, whether around plain or patterned cushions.

ABOVE: There are endless possibilities for decorative finishes on gathered or pleated frills.

Flat-bordered cushions

Flat-bordered cushions are ideal for adding decorative interest while retaining a tailored plainness. There are a few variations of this style. Again, a good average size is from 35 cm × 35 cm (14 in × 14 in) to 40 cm × 40 cm (16 in × 16 in) with a 4 cm to 6 cm (1½ in to 2¼ in) border.

A single flat border

MEASURING

Measure the inner pad from seam to seam across the centre and add the required width of the border plus 1.5 cm (⅝ in) seam allowance to all four sides. Transfer measurements to fabric or make a paper pattern.

Example: for 30 cm (12 in) sq cushion with a 6 cm (2¼ in) border: 1.5 + 6 + 30 + 6 + 1.5 = 45 cm (⅝ + 2¼ + 12 + 2¼ + ⅝ = 17¾ in), so pattern will be 45 cm (approx 18 in) sq. (Add 3 cm [1¼ in] to width of back for zip opening.)

REQUIREMENTS

Paper pattern
Fabric for front and back, plus extra for border (p. 18)
Zip: 4 cm (1½ in) shorter than width of inner pad
Inner pad

METHOD FOR A SQUARE CUSHION COVER

1. *Cut out front and back cover for cushion cover according to pattern.*
2. *Make up the cushion cover back with a zip in the centre* (p. 12).
3. *Position right sides and raw edges of front and back together (zip open), and sew 1.5 cm (⅝ in) from edge right round the cover. Clip corners, turn right side out, and press seam edge neatly.*
4. *Measure and mark sewing line on front cover 4 cm to 6 cm (1½ to 2¼ in) (or required width of border) in from edge on all four sides, using tailors' chalk.*

PADDED BORDER *If you want the border to be firm and padded, you can work flat strips of wadding (batting), 2 cm (¾ in) wider than the width of the border, in with the seam. These strips will be sandwiched between the front and the back when the cover is turned through.*

5. *You can now either:*
❏ *sew a single straight line on this marked line right round cover through all thicknesses, or*
❏ *Use sewing machine's decorative satin stitch and embroidery cotton and sew once or twice round cover along this line (Fig. 15). (If you have inserted wadding (batting), the lower end of it is caught in this sewing.)*
6. *Insert inner pad.*

Fig. 15

OPPOSITE: A feminine bedroom in pinks and greens with a four-poster bed draped in chintz mock curtains and valance, which are decorated with a frill edging. A gathered bed valance in broderie anglaise lace, a shaped dressing table with a contrasting back frill and a narrower front frill edging the loose cover, and pretty scatter cushions with frills complete the picture.

A double flat border

MEASURING

Measure the inner pad from seam to seam across the centre. Add the desired finished width of the border (× 2) plus 1.5 cm (⅝ in) seam allowance to all four sides. Cut out paper pattern.

Example: for 30 cm (12 in) sq cushion with a 6 cm (2¼ in) border: 1.5 + 6 + 6 + 30 + 6 + 6 + 1.5 = 57 cm, so pattern will be 57 cm (approx 23 in) sq. (Add 3 cm [1¼ in] to width of back for zip opening.)

REQUIREMENTS

Paper pattern
Fabric for front and back, plus extra for border (p. 18)
Zip: 4 cm (1½ in) shorter than width of cushion pad
Inner pad

METHOD FOR A SQUARE CUSHION COVER

1. Cut out cushion cover front and back according to paper pattern.
2. Make up the cushion cover back with zip opening in centre (p. 12).
3. On both front and back pieces, fold width of border (4 cm to 6 cm [1½ in to 2¼ in]) plus seam allowance to inside on all four sides, and press (Fig. 16a). *Open out again.*
4. Follow steps 2–4 (pp. 68–69) *for mitring corners on a hem. Figure 16a also shows how each corner is folded to the inside to meet the intersection of the inner fold lines* (step 2, p. 68).
5. Pin front to back, wrong sides together. Measure and mark sewing line on cushion cover front the required width of border (4 cm to 6 cm [1½ in to 2¼ in]) in from edge on all four sides, using tailors' chalk.
6. Sew along this marked line once or twice right round the cover. You may use a decorative satin stitch and matching or contrasting embroidery cotton (Fig. 16b; Fig. 15, p. 20). *Insert inner pad.*

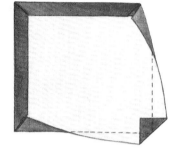

Fig. 16a   Fig. 16b

A double flat contrasting border

MEASURING

Measure and make pattern according to instructions for a cushion with a single flat border *(p. 20)*.

REQUIREMENTS

Paper pattern
Fabric for front and back (p. 18)
Contrast fabric for front and back border (p. 18)
Zip: 4 cm (1½ in) shorter than width of cushion pad
Inner pad

METHOD FOR A SQUARE CUSHION COVER

1. Cut out cushion cover front and back according to paper pattern.
2. Make up cushion cover back with zip in centre (p. 12).
3. Cut out front and back of border according to paper pattern.
4. On each of the two pieces of contrast fabric, mark a cutting line in from the edge, the width of the border plus 3 cm (1¼ in), on all four sides. Carefully cut along this line on both pieces of fabric (Fig. 17a). *You will now have two fabric frames* (Fig. 17b). *Alternatively, the frame can be made with strips of fabric, the width of the border plus*

 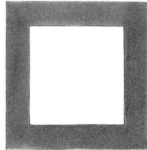

Fig. 17a   Fig. 17b

3 cm (1¼ in), joined with mitred corners (Fig. 17c). The latter method would be very effective when using a striped fabric as the contrast.

5. *With right sides together, pin one frame on cushion front. Stitch right round, allowing a 1.5 cm (⅝ in) seam (Fig. 17d). Cut corners. Turn out, push out corners, and press seam neatly. Repeat this step for cushion back.*

6. *To complete, repeat steps 5 and 6 for cushion cover with double flat border (p. 22).*

 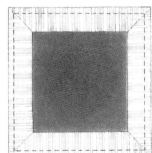

Fig. 17c   Fig. 17d

HINT *The cushion front can be made a few centimetres smaller than the back. The contrast at the back would then be visible as it frames the front border.*

ABOVE: These comfortable seat and back-rest cushions have piping in the centre seam and gathered corners.

BOLSTERS

These cushions with their pleasing, fat sausage shapes were traditionally used to bolster pillows on a bed. Today, apart from their decorative interest, bolster cushions offer practical solutions to seating areas where extra back or arm support is needed. Fabrics with a directional design, such as stripes, geometric patterns and trellises, are particularly suited to the style of this cushion and can be used vertically or horizontally. Solid foam can be cut to size for the bolster pad. The covers are made with zip openings so that they can be removed for cleaning.

Piped bolster

MEASURING

Make a rectangular paper pattern using the length and circumference of the bolster and adding a 1.5 cm (⅝ in) seam allowance all round. Make a round pattern for the circular ends using the bolster diameter (see instructions for making a pattern for a round cushion cover on page 11), and adding a 1.5 cm (⅝ in) seam allowance all round *(Fig. 18)*.

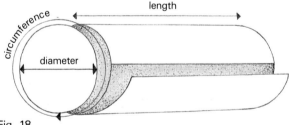

Fig. 18

REQUIREMENTS
Paper pattern: 1 rectangular piece and 2 round pieces
Fabric
Piping: enough to go round ends of bolster plus a bit extra for joining
Zip: 10 cm (4 in) shorter than the length of the bolster
Bolster pad of solid foam

METHOD

1. *Cut out fabric according to pattern. Take main fabric piece (the large rectangle) and sew a line of stitching on the seam line of both short ends. Clip into seam allowance at regular intervals (Fig. 19a).*

Fig. 19a

2. *With right sides together, fold main fabric piece in half lengthwise, and sew 5 cm (2 in) in on both ends (1.5 cm [⅝ in] seam allowance) (Fig. 19b). Tack opening closed along seam line, and insert zip (steps 3 and 4, pp. 11–12). You will now have a tube.*

3. *Unpick tacking, open zip, and turn tube inside out.*

Fig. 19b

4. *Clip into piping seam allowance at regular intervals, then tack and sew piping to right sides of two round pieces (Fig. 19c).*

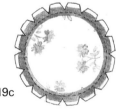

Fig. 19c

5. *With right sides and raw edges together, pin, tack and sew circles to ends of tube* (Fig. 19d). *Trim seams, turn right side out, and press. Insert bolster pad.*

Fig. 19d

ABOVE: A gathered end bolster cushion, a plain piped cushion and a contrasting flat-bordered cushion lie on top of a piped boxed cushion.

Gathered end bolster

MEASURING
This bolster is made from a single rectangular piece of fabric, the length being the length of the bolster plus the diameter plus 3 cm (1¼ in), and the width being the circumference of the bolster plus 3 cm (1¼ in) *(p. 24)*. You shouldn't need to make a pattern for this bolster.

REQUIREMENTS
Fabric
Bolster pad of solid foam
Covered button (or cardboard disc)

METHOD
1. *With right sides together, fold fabric in half lengthwise, and sew a 1.5 cm (⅝ in) seam across. Press seam open. Press a 1.5 cm (⅝ in) hem towards inside at both ends.*
2. *Turn right side out, and hand-stitch two rows of gathering stitches at each end (Fig. 20a).*
3. *Insert bolster pad into the tube so that you have equal ends over at each side.*
4. *Pull up gathering stitches at each end tightly, and distribute gathers evenly. Tie off gathering threads, and back-stitch them securely (Fig. 20b).*
5. *Cover two buttons (Fig. 20c) (according to the manufacturer's instructions), position over gathers, and sew in place in centre on both ends.*

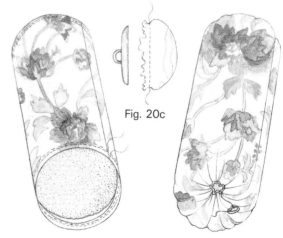

Fig. 20c

Fig. 20a

Fig. 20b

Bolster with knotted end

This is a fun and easy way to finish off the front end of a bolster that serves as an armrest on a sofa. The other end, which faces the back of the sofa, is plain.

MEASURING

A rectangle of fabric is used with a round piece sewn on at one end. The length of the rectangle is the length of the bolster pad plus about three-quarters of this length again. The width is the circumference of the bolster pad plus 3 cm (1¼ in). The round piece is the diameter of the circular end of the bolster pad plus a 1.5 cm (⅝ in) seam allowance all round *(p. 24)*.

REQUIREMENTS

Pattern: 1 rectangular piece and 1 round piece
Fabric
Binding or lace: the length of short side of rectangular piece plus a bit extra for overlapping
Bolster pad of solid foam

METHOD

1. *Sew a row of stitching on seam line of one short side of rectangle, and clip into seam allowance* (Fig. 21a). *Sew binding or lace to raw edge of other end according to instructions on page 66.*

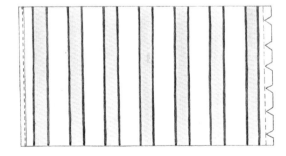

Fig. 21a

2. *With right sides together, fold in half lengthwise and join two long edges of rectangle. Press seam flat.*
3. *Attach round piece to the clipped end of tube, right sides together. Clip into the seam allowance of round piece. Turn right side out* (Fig. 21b).
4. *Insert bolster pad. Tie the overhanging piece of fabric into a knot, centring it as close to the end of the bolster pad as possible.*

size of bolster pad

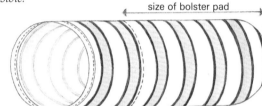

Fig. 21b

ABOVE: A flat-bordered cushion with decorative piping lies against a bolster with a knotted end.

OPPOSITE: Comfort to sink away in — plump back-rest cushions with rounded, gathered corners; a boxed cushion with piping; knotted end bolsters as armrests; and pretty flat-bordered scatter cushions decorate this wooden bench.

Bolster-style neck cushion

This is a much smaller version of a bolster cushion and is mentioned here because its shape is similar to that of a bolster cushion. The inner pad is not a firm piece of foam, but is made of lining which is stuffed with any of the soft fillings you can use for scatter cushions *(p. 10)*. Because of its sausage shape and softness, it is an ideal neck cushion. It is also feminine and decorative, and looks pretty amongst a scatter of different cushions on a bed. They would look lovely next to a boxed cushion to give a pleasing contrast of cushion shapes.

This little cushion has a nostalgic story to it. One of our great-grandmothers used one, and I have vivid memories of her lying on her bed against some pillows with this dainty white cushion tucked behind her neck for extra comfort and support. It was made for her by her daughter, who then passed the pattern on to me.

Making the inner pad

The inner pad is made from a piece of lining measuring 36 cm × 39 cm (14¼ in × 15½ in) and two round ends each measuring 15 cm (6 in) in diameter. Make up as for piped bolster *(pp. 24–25)* omitting the piping and the zip, but leaving an opening where the zip would be. The seam allowance is 1.5 cm (⅝ in). Stuff with a filling of your choice, and slip-stitch the opening closed.

Making the cover

REQUIREMENTS

Rectangular piece of fabric: 41 cm × 49 cm (16¼ in × 19½ in)
2 strips of fabric for frills: each 9 cm × 85 cm (3½ in × 34 in) (optional: use broderie anglaise lace)
2 strips of lace or bias binding: each 85 cm (34 in) long (optional)
2 strips of border fabric: each 42 cm (16½ in) long
2 satin ribbons for drawstrings: each 50 cm (20 in) long
Velcro strips

METHOD

1. *Overlock or zigzag raw edges of rectangle right round.*
2. *Make hem by turning under 2 cm (¾ in) on each long side. Press and sew.*
3. *Make casings on short sides by turning under 2 cm (¾ in). Press and sew (Fig. 22a).*

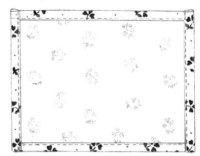

Fig. 22a

4. *Mark a line on the right side, 7 cm (2¾ in) in from both short ends (Fig. 22b).*

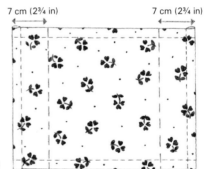

7 cm (2¾ in)   7 cm (2¾ in)

Fig. 22b

5. *On each frill strip, finish three raw edges with a 5 mm (¼ in) hem (or sew lace to edge). Sew gathering stitches along remaining long raw edges, and draw in each frill to measure 44 cm (17½ in).*
6. *Press in raw edges of long sides of border strips to display pattern on right side neatly. Fold and press in 1 cm (⅜ in) on each short end (Fig. 22c).*

7. *Position and pin border on marked line of fabric with gathered frill in between* (Fig. 22d). *Sew both sides of border in place. Repeat on other side* (Fig. 22e).

Fig. 22c

Fig. 22d

Fig. 22e

8. *Sew Velcro strips to long sides of cover to close* (Fig. 22f).
9. *Thread ribbons through casings* (Fig. 22f).
10. *Fold cover around inner pad, fasten Velcro strips, draw in ribbons at each end, and make bows* (Fig. 22f).

Fig. 22f

BOXED CUSHIONS

The term 'boxed cushion' refers to a firm, three-dimensional foam inner pad that is covered with fabric. These cushions are generally used as seat cushions on cane and wicker furniture or in bay windows and can, in fact, turn many hard surfaces into comfortable extra seating space.

The best way to cover a boxed cushion is to accommodate the depth of the cushion by means of a gusset. A zip is inserted into the gusset so that the cushion cover can be removed and washed. Piping along the top and bottom seams provides a crisp, neat finish. Foam inner pads can be cut to any size and shape.

Square boxed cushion with piping

MEASURING

Measure width and length of top of foam inner pad, add 1.5 cm (⅝ in) seam allowance all round, and make a paper pattern (A) using these measurements. Measure length and height of one side of foam inner pad, add 1.5 cm (⅝ in) seam allowance all round, and make a pattern (B) using these measurements. Make another pattern (C), using measurements from pattern B and adding on 3 cm (1¼ in) to the height (short side). *(Fig. 23a.)*

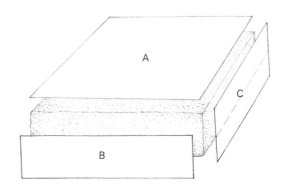

Fig. 23a

Alternatively, the gusset for the three sides can be made out of a continuous strip of fabric measuring the total length of the three sides by the height, plus 1.5 cm (⅝ in) seam allowance all round. Pattern C for the fourth side will remain the same.

REQUIREMENTS
Paper pattern: A, B and C
Fabric
Zip: 5 cm (2 in) shorter than pattern C
Piping: to go 2 × round all sides plus a bit extra for joining
Square foam inner pad

METHOD
1. *Cut out the following pieces of fabric:*
    2 × pattern A
    3 × pattern B (or one continuous strip
      as described above)
    1 × pattern C
2. *Cut piece C in half lengthwise, and with right sides of cut edges together, sew in from each side, leaving an opening for the zip. Insert zip* (steps 3 and 4, pp. 11–12).
3. *With right sides together, sew 1.5 cm (⅝ in) seams, joining short sides of four gusset strips together, but leaving 1.5 cm (⅝ in) open at the top and bottom of each seam. Secure by back-stitching at both ends* (Fig. 23b).

1.5 cm (⅝ in) opening

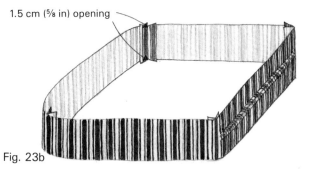

Fig. 23b

4. *Pin and tack piping to right sides of top and bottom pieces, making sure that the piping joins at the back of the cushion. Clip piping at corners. Join ends of piping neatly* (p. 66).
5. *With right sides and raw edges together, pin and tack gusset to bottom piece of fabric, matching corners to seams on gusset and turning gusset sharply at the corners* (Fig. 23c). *Sew in place.*
6. *With zip open, repeat step 5 for top piece. Trim seams, clip corners, turn right side out, and press. Insert foam inner pad.*

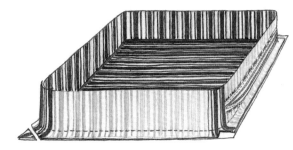

Fig. 23c

Rectangular boxed cushion

A rectangular boxed cushion is made in the same way as a square boxed cushion, with long and short gusset strips cut according to the side measurements. One of the long gusset strips must accommodate the zip, which should be three-quarters of the length of the strip.

OPPOSITE: Gathered end bolsters, a piped boxed cushion and a group of contrasting double flat-bordered and piped scatter cushions create a cosy seat in the sun. The table-cloth, in matching fabric, has a very wide frill edging.

Round boxed cushion

MEASURING
Measure the diameter of the foam inner pad, add 1.5 cm (⅝ in) seam allowance all round, and make a round paper pattern (A) using these measurements *(p. 11)*. Measure the circumference and the height of the foam inner pad, and make a paper pattern (B) with the length two-thirds of the circumference by the height, plus 1.5 cm (⅝ in) seam allowance all round. Make a pattern (C) with the length one-third of the circumference by the height, plus 1.5 cm (⅝ in) seam allowance all round, plus 3 cm (1¼ in) to the height (short side).

REQUIREMENTS
Paper pattern: A, B and C
Fabric
Piping: 2 × the circumference plus a bit extra
Zip: 5 cm (2 in) shorter than long side of pattern C
Round foam inner pad

METHOD
1. *Cut out the following pieces of fabric:*
   2 × pattern A
   1 × pattern B
   1 × pattern C
2. *Cut C in half lengthwise, and with right sides of cut edges together, sew a 1.5 cm (⅝ in) seam from each side, leaving central opening for zip. Insert zip (steps 3 and 4, pp. 11–12).*
3. *With right sides together, join gusset pieces (B and C) with 1.5 cm (⅝ in) seams.*
4. *Sew a line of stitching round the top and bottom edge of the gusset on the seam line. Clip into seam allowance at regular intervals to allow for ease when attaching the top and the bottom pieces (Fig. 24).*
5. *Pin and tack piping to right sides of top and bottom pieces (A), clipping into piping seam allowance at regular intervals (Fig. 24). Join ends of piping (p. 66).*

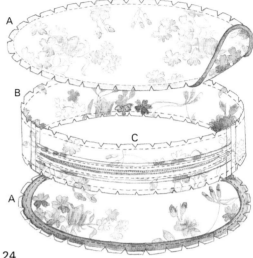

Fig. 24

6. *With right sides and raw edges together, pin and tack the gusset to the top piece of fabric and sew. Repeat, with zip open, on the bottom piece. Trim seams, turn right side out, and press. Insert foam inner pad.*

Shaped boxed cushion

The same method applies to making shaped boxed cushions. Take templates from the foam inner pad and proceed to make patterns, remembering always to add your 1.5 cm (⅝ in) seam allowances. Ensure that the zip opening on the gusset is positioned on the widest part of the cushion and that it is big enough to insert the foam pad.

OPPOSITE: A fantasy bedroom for a girl with a cream dream quilt, cream curtains and valances with frills on a four-poster, and scatter cushions decorated with ribbon, lace and pin-tucks.

OVERLEAF: A romantic bedroom with fabric draped over a wooden frame suspended from the ceiling.

PART TWO

COVERS FOR BEDROOMS

A bedroom is essentially a private space, a place of refuge and retreat from the outside world, a room for rest and rejuvenation. Tastes in bedroom decorating may vary considerably, but the aim should always be towards creating an atmosphere of soothing serenity.

It is the one room in a house that should be decorated to please yourself and, if you so wish, indulge your fantasies. If you share your bedroom with a partner, you will have to consider another person's needs and preferences. It seems to me that most men have accepted, and are tolerant of, the fact that women tend to decorate bedrooms to suit their feminine tastes. If your partner, however, dislikes frills and flounces, opt for a tailored, more constrained look, using a combination of striped

geometric and traditional prints in 'masculine' colours to create a room of stunning simplicity.

The bed is the largest piece of furniture in the room, and is thus an important element in bedroom decorating. Other elements are side tables with table-cloths, a bed valance and duvet or bedspread, and to finish off, a scatter of pretty cushions against the pillows. Brass, iron and wooden bed frames and four-posters give the bed even more importance in a room and provide a wonderful opportunity for creative decorating, whether simple or elaborate. Whatever the choice of bed dressing, there should be a harmonious relationship with the decoration of the rest of the room and all should integrate and co-ordinate to create the restful ambience so important in a bedroom.

CONTINENTAL PILLOWCASES

Continental pillows are large and square, and are traditionally used with a duvet and a bed valance to create a look that we have become familiar with, although it is 'borrowed' from the European continent. In our bedrooms, the continental pillow is most often used to decorate the top end of a bed rather than for sleeping on. The pillowcase is made to match or co-ordinate with the duvet cover and bed valance in choice of colour and decorative style.

Continental pillowcases may be plain, especially if they are going to be slept on, in which case the only decoration need be a contrasting piping, or piping and a frill. Flat-bordered pillowcases are also very attractive and practical. To make them, follow the instructions for making flat-bordered scatter cushions on pages 20–23.

For a more decorative look, the front of the pillowcase can be attractively adorned with strips of binding and borders or a combination of pin-tucks, lace and ribbon. The suggestions for different frills and edgings for scatter cushions *(p. 19)* can all be used on continental pillowcases.

Piped continental pillowcase with a frill

MEASURING

Measure the width and the length of the pillow across the centre (a continental pillow is usually square), and add a 1.5 cm (⅝ in) seam allowance all round. The measurement of the flap pocket should be 20 cm (8 in) by the full width of the cushion. Use the formula on page 69 to work out how much fabric you will need for the frill.

REQUIREMENTS
Fabric for back and front
Fabric for frill: 10 cm (4 in) strips for a single frill *(p. 69)*
Piping: enough to go round 4 sides plus a bit extra for joining
Fabric for flap pocket

METHOD

1. *Follow instructions on pages 17–18 (steps 3–7) to make and attach the frill and piping to the front of the pillowcase (Fig. 25a).*
2. *Sew a double 1 cm (⅜ in) hem along one of the sides of the back of the pillowcase. Sew a double 1 cm (⅜ in) hem along one of the long sides of the flap pocket.*

Fig. 25a

3. *With right sides and raw edges together, pin and tack the flap pocket over the back piece, onto the front piece (right sides and raw edges of front and back together) so that the edge of the hem on the back piece aligns with the seam line of the front piece (Fig. 25b).*
4. *Stitch round the four sides of the cover (Fig. 25b), turn right side out, and press.*

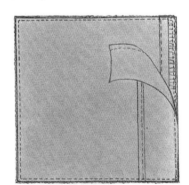

Fig. 25b

BED VALANCES

A bed valance covers the unattractive base of a bed. Whether used with a duvet or a bedspread, it provides an opportunity to introduce a contrast fabric to co-ordinate with the rest of the fabric mix in the bedroom. Valances in striped fabrics emphasize the crisp, neat lines of a bed. For a feminine look, the frill may be gathered; for a masculine look, it can be box-pleated; or for a tailored finish, the sides can be straight with deep inverted pleats at the bottom corners.

The basic method for making these valances is the same. The flat piece covering the base of the bed is made out of lining, with a strip of fabric in the same fabric as the frill bordering its outer edge and hiding all the seams.

Gathered bed valance

MEASURING

Careful and accurate measuring is the key to a neat, well-fitting end product. Measure the length and the width of the base of the bed across the centre. The height is measured from the edge of the base of the bed to the floor *(Fig. 26)*.

Fig. 26

WORKING OUT HOW MUCH FABRIC YOU WILL NEED
1. *For lining, use measurements for length and width of base of bed and add 1.5 cm (⅝ in) seam allowance all round.*
2. *For border, use two strips of fabric 15 cm (6 in) wide by length of base, plus 1.5 cm (⅝ in) seam allowance all round; and one strip of fabric 15 cm (6 in) wide by width of base, plus 1.5 cm (⅝ in) seam allowance all round.*

3. *Use the following formula to work out how much fabric you will need for the frill: (2 × length of base + 1 × width of base) × 2. Divide by 150 (the fabric width) to determine how many widths of fabric are needed (pattern match if necessary; p. 69). Multiply the number of widths by the height of the bed plus 6.5 cm (2½ in) (5 cm [2 in] for hem + 1.5 cm [⅝ in] seam allowance for top).*

METHOD

1. *To join the strips of fabric for the border, mitre the corners (p. 68) and leave 2 cm (¾ in) free on insides of corners. Ensure that this 'frame' fits the lining exactly (Fig. 27a).*
2. *Press a 1.5 cm (⅝ in) hem to the wrong side along the inside of the 'frame' (Fig. 27a).*
3. *Divide the total measurement of the two sides plus the bottom end of the lining into six. Starting at one top corner, mark this measurement along the three edges of the lining where the frill will be attached (Fig. 27b).*
4. *Join the fabric widths for the frill, and pattern match if necessary.*

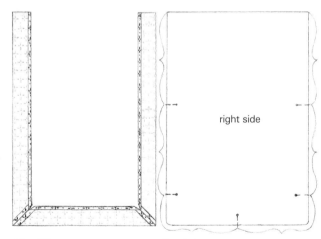

right side

Fig. 27a   Fig. 27b

5. *Along one long edge of the frill, press in a 5 mm (¼ in) hem, then a 4.5 cm (1¾ in) hem, and sew.*

6. *Fold the frill into six equal sections and mark each fold with tailors' chalk (or pins). Prepare for gathering up each section between these marks by zigzagging over a strong thread like perlé or crochet cotton (Fig. 27c).*

7. *With wrong side of ungathered frill facing wrong side of lining, and raw edges even, pin corresponding marks on lining and frill together, and gather the frill in sections to fit the marked-off sections on the lining (Fig. 27d). Secure ends of gathering threads by winding them around pins, and pin and tack the frill into position. Sew a 1.5 cm (⅝ in) seam around the three sides.*

8. *With right side of border 'frame' to right side of frill, and raw edges together, pin, tack and sew on previous seam line (Fig. 27d).*

9. *Trim corners and seams, and fold border to right side. Press. Sew folded hem of border to lining (Fig. 27e).*

10. *Turn the raw edges at the top end of the frill and lining over twice, and sew this hem (Fig. 27f).*

Fig. 27d

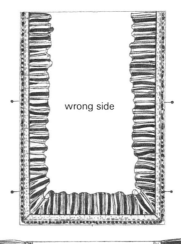

wrong side

Fig. 27e

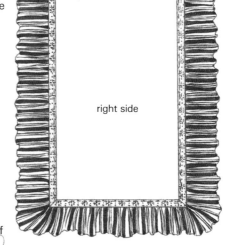

right side

Fig. 27c

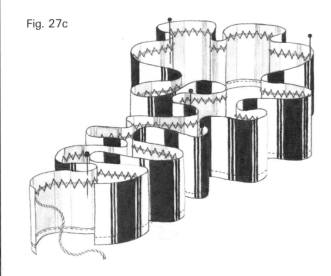

Fig. 27f

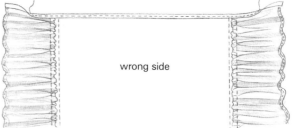

wrong side

Ideas for decorative finishes on gathered bed valances

The pretty, feminine style of the gathered bed valance lends itself to the ornate treatment of adding lace, ribbons and pin-tucks. These must be added in horizontal lines along the length of the frill before it is gathered. Another option for opulent dressing-up of a gathered valance is to use a 30 cm (12 in) wide broderie anglaise lace as a frill or as a top layer over a plain or patterned fabric underneath. Lace fabric can also be used in the same way, and even scooped up at regular intervals to create soft swags.

ABOVE: The valance on this brass bed is split at the bottom corners and tied with decorative bows.

NOTE *A gathered or box-pleated valance for a wooden- or iron-framed bed should be split at the corners. Measure carefully to determine exactly where this split should be. Bands of fabric can be sewn on at each side of the split and tied around the bottom posts into decorative bows.*

Box-pleated bed valance

The same instructions apply here as for a gathered valance, except the length of the frill is calculated as follows: three times the total measurement of the two sides of the bed plus the width of the bottom end of the base of the bed *(Fig. 26, p. 37)*. The height is the same as before. The hem should be sewn before the pleats are pressed in.

A good average size for a pleat is 10 cm (4 in). It is important, though, that the outer edges of two adjoining pleats should meet on each of the two corners. To attain this, divide the width of the bed into equally sized pleats as close to 10 cm (4 in) as possible (for example, a double bed 137 cm [4 ft 6 in] wide will have fourteen pleats at the bottom, measuring 9.79 cm [just under 4 in] each). Make a template out of cardboard equal to the width and the length of the pleat and use it to mark out the pleats in tailors' chalk on the wrong side of the fabric *(Fig. 28a)*. Fold line A to line C, line B to line D, line F to line D, line E to line G, and so on, all along the frill *(Fig. 28b)*. Pin and tack the pleats in position as you go along, and press when finished. Position the centre pleat(s) of the frill to the centre of the lining across the

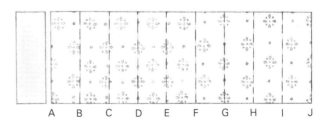

A   B   C   D   E   F   G   H   I   J

Fig. 28a

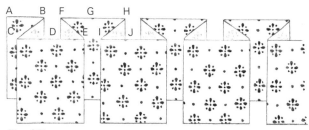

Fig. 28b

Position any joins so that they will fall to the inside of the pleat. Measure and fold the pleats into position *(Fig. 29a)*. Press and tack down. Proceed as before to join the frill to the lining and to finish off with a border strip. (See *steps 7–9, p. 38*). A 3 cm to 5 cm (1¼ in to 2 in) contrasting border or a broad strip of cotton lace along the edge of a valance with straight sides would also add an interesting finishing touch. Figure 29b shows how the above method can be adapted to make a divan cover.

width *(Fig. 28c)*, and attach the frill to the lining as before *(step 7, p. 38)*, ensuring that the outer edges of two adjoining pleats meet at each corner *(Fig. 28c)*. Finish off with border strip as before *(steps 8 and 9, p. 38)*.

To add a touch of definition to the strict geometric quality of a box-pleated valance, a contrast border may be sewn on at the hem. One or two rows of contrasting binding will be a very effective trim if sewn on a few centimetres up from the hem and a few centimetres apart.

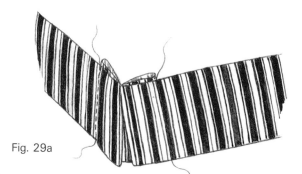

Fig. 29a

Fig. 29b

Fig. 28c

Bed valance with straight sides and inverted pleats on each corner

The same instructions apply here as for the gathered valance *(p. 37)*, except the length of the frill is calculated as follows: the width of the base of the bed plus twice the length plus 80 cm (32 in) for each inverted pleat (this will result in a 20 cm [8 in] deep pleat on each side of the corner).

DUVET COVERS

Duvets, or continental quilts, originated on the European continent and have become internationally popular because they suit our modern 'low-maintenance' lifestyle so well. Apart from being practical, duvet covers have become an important part of bedroom decorating and are made in fabrics to co-ordinate with valances, curtains and furniture.

Although there is a good range of ready-made duvet covers in the shops, not only can you save money by making your own, but you can use the fabric of your choice in the pattern and colour that exactly matches the decor of your bedroom. The best fabric to use is a pure cotton.

Pure cotton breathes and washes well, but needs a bit more care when washing and ironing. If you dislike the slightly rougher texture of the fabric against your skin, you can use sheeting in a matching colour for the underside of the duvet (as long as its washing qualities are compatible with the cotton). Or, if you do make your cover reversible, you may choose to use it with a top sheet on your bed. This also saves the cover from having to be washed so often. Incidentally, the fabric will become softer with washing.

A duvet cover is very easy to make, being really just a big fabric bag. Piping defines the edges, and piping and a frill add a pretty, feminine touch. The top of the duvet cover may be decorated with pin-tucks, ribbon and lace, or bands of border strips and binding, or even patchwork. But remember that a duvet cover used in the traditional way is washed regularly. So, keep your decorating practical, or use your duvet cover with a top sheet.

> **HINT** *Make a design feature of the duvet cover opening. Position the opening at the bottom of the bed, and use three or four matching or contrasting bow ties (evenly spaced) as a fastening. (See* Side opening with bows *on pages 14–15 for a method for using bow ties as a fastening.)*

Basic duvet cover

MEASURING
There are three standard sizes for duvets:
Single: 135 cm × 200 cm (54 in × 78 in)
Double: 200 cm × 200 cm (78 in × 78 in)
King: 230 cm × 220 cm (90 in × 86 in)

It is wise, though, to measure your duvet across the width and the length as a check. However, it is common to have a king-size duvet on a double bed — it's a matter of personal preference. Add 2 cm (¾ in) to the top and two sides, and 8 cm (3¼ in) to the bottom end for the front and back of the cover. (Use two widths if the duvet is wider than 150 cm [60 in]).

REQUIREMENTS
Fabric for the front
Fabric or sheeting for the back
Press-stud tape or Velcro

METHOD
1. *Cut out fabric for front and back. Join widths, if necessary, to make up to the required size by adding equal pieces of second width to both sides of first width. Pattern match if necessary* (p. 69).
2. *Sew a double 2.5 cm (1 in) hem along the bottom edge of front and back pieces.*
3. *Position front on back with right sides together, and sew in 30 cm (12 in) from each side at the bottom just under the hems, leaving a central opening* (Fig. 30a).
4. *Cut the press-stud tape or Velcro 3 cm (1¼ in) longer than the opening. Separate and stitch a strip to each hem along the opening, ensuring that the corresponding studs or Velcro strips align* (Fig. 30b). *Turn cover right side out.*
5. *To enclose raw edges of the tape at each side of the opening, stitch vertically across the hems* (Fig. 30c). *Sew again for strength.*

Fig. 30a

Fig. 30b

Fig. 30c

REQUIREMENTS
Fabric for the front and back
Broderie anglaise lace: 2 × width
Press-studs

METHOD

1. *Repeat step 1 on page 41.*

2. *Sew a small double hem at the top of the front and back pieces.*

3. *Sew a strip of broderie anglaise lace across top of back piece (right side), with scallops just over hem. Sew a second strip of lace to cover stitching of first (Fig. 31a).*

4. *Fold 30 cm (12 in) of the decorated top end over to the right side (Fig. 31b).*

5. *With right sides and raw edges together, position front on back. Sew a 1.5 cm (⅝ in) seam along three edges (Fig. 31c).*

6. *To make French seams on remaining sides of the cover, pin wrong sides and raw edges together, tack and sew down the two long sides, allowing 1 cm (⅜ in) for seams. Trim seams to 5 mm (¼ in), and clip corners. Turn through, and, with right sides together, sew again round the two sides. Do the same along top edge. Turn right side out, and press.*

Decorated flap pocket for duvet cover

This style of duvet cover does away with any method of fastening. The cover is made in the same way as a pillowcase, with the flap pocket to the outside, at the top. The flap is decorated with rows of lace, and, for a more luxurious trimming, pin-tucks and ribbon.

MEASURING

For the front, use the width and length measurement of the duvet *(p. 41)* and add a 1.5 cm (⅝ in) seam allowance all round. For the back, add 30 cm (12 in) to the length of the measurement for the front.

ABOVE: The flap pocket at the top of this duvet cover is decorated with two rows of cream broderie anglaise lace.

6. *Turn right side out, and then turn flap pocket over to the front. Press all seams.*

7. *Sew a few press-studs under the edge of the flap pocket and to their corresponding positions on the front of the duvet cover (Fig. 31d).*

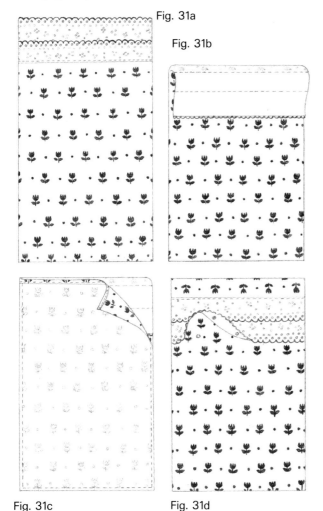

Fig. 31a

Fig. 31b

Fig. 31c

Fig. 31d

Piped duvet cover with a frill

MEASURING

For the front, use the width and length measurements of the basic duvet cover *(p. 41)* and add a 1.5 cm (⅝ in) seam allowance all round. (Use two widths if duvet is wider than 150 cm [60 in].) For the back, use the width and length measurements of the basic duvet cover *(p. 41)*. Add a 1.5 cm (⅝ in) seam allowance to the top and the two sides, and 8 cm (3¼ in) to the bottom end. (Use two widths if necessary.)

> **HINT** *To ensure comfort, the opening should be at the bottom end of the bed. If you find this unattractive on a reversible duvet cover, position the opening at the top.*

The ungathered frill must be 2¼ times the combined length of the four sides (or three sides if you leave the top plain) *(p. 69)*. For a single frill, you will need 10 cm (4 in) strips; for a double frill, you will need 18 cm (7 in) strips. A reversible duvet cover must have a double frill *(p. 19)*.

REQUIREMENTS
Fabric for the front and back and the frill
Piping: enough to go round 4 sides plus a bit
extra for joining
A strip of fabric for binding: 8 cm (3¼ in) wide and as
long as the width of the duvet
Press-stud tape or Velcro

METHOD
1. *Cut out fabric for front and back of duvet cover, and join widths to make up required sizes by adding equal pieces of second width to both sides of first width (see* Fig. 33b, p. 45 *for an illustration of this).*
2. *Sew a double 2.5 cm (1 in) hem along the bottom edge of the back piece.*

3. *With right sides and raw edges together, pin and tack piping right round the front piece (step 3, p. 16).*

4. *Join the strips of fabric for the frill using French seams (step 6, p. 42) to form a large circle. On a single frill, finish one raw edge with a small double hem; for a double frill, fold in half lengthwise. Fold frill into eight equal sections and mark the folds. Prepare for gathering up each section by zigzagging over perlé or crochet cotton between these marks (Fig. 13b, p. 17).*

5. *Divide the total measurement of the sides of the cover that the frill will be attached to into eight equal sections. Starting at one corner of the cover, mark this measurement off with tailors' chalk (or use pins) (Fig. 27b, p. 37).*

6. *With right sides and raw edges together, pin the corresponding marks on the duvet and ungathered frill together, and gather frill in sections to fit the marked-off sections of the top of the cover. Secure ends of gathering thread by winding it round pins, and pin and sew the frill into position.*

7. *Bind the raw edges at the bottom end with the strip of binding fabric (Fig. 32).*

Fig. 32

8. *Position front on back with right sides together, and sew in 30 cm (12 in) from each side at the bottom, just under previous stitching lines, leaving a central opening. Repeat steps 4 and 5 on page 41.*

9. *With right sides and raw edges together, stitch the remaining three sides. Neaten seams and zigzag over raw edges. Turn right side out, and press.*

BEDCOVERS

The most popular style of bedcover is the throw-over bedspread. It can be lined, quilted or made of patchwork. It either hangs right down to the floor on three sides of a bed, or covers the mattress and a little bit of the bed valance. The bottom corners of the throw-over are rounded to hang neatly at the corners of a bed. If a bed has a simple or ornate wooden or metal frame, the throw-over is then tucked in under the mattress at the foot end.

ABOVE: Pin-tucks, ribbon and lace decorate the cushions on this white dream quilt.

Lined throw-over bedspread with piping

This is the simplest bedcover to make. The same method applies whether using fabric on both sides for a reversible cover or lining at the back for a less expensive alternative.

MEASURING

Decide on whether the bedspread should hang down to the floor or just cover the mattress. Take the relevant width and length measurements over a made-up bed *(Fig. 33a)*, and add a 2 cm (¾ in) seam allowance to all four sides.

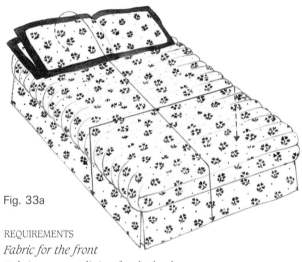

Fig. 33a

REQUIREMENTS
Fabric for the front
Fabric or cotton lining for the back
Piping: enough to go round 4 sides plus a bit extra for joining

---

HINT *When calculating how much fabric you will need for a bedspread, remember that if the required width of the bedspread is more than 150 cm (60 in), you will need two widths each for the front and back. Remember to take pattern repeats into account (p. 69).*

METHOD

1. *Repeat step 1 on page 43.*
2. *Round the two corners at the bottom ends of the front and back of the cover (Fig. 33b).*

Fig. 33b

3. *With raw edges together, pin and tack piping to right side of front cover.*
4. *With right sides and raw edges together, pin and tack the back cover to the front cover. Sew right round, leaving a 50 cm (20 in) opening at the top end. Trim seams, notch the seam allowance of the curved corners, turn right side out, and press.*
5. *Slip-stitch opening closed, or top-stitch 1 cm (⅜ in) from the edge right round.*

Throw-over bedspread made of ready-made quilted fabric

Ready-quilted fabrics are ideal for making up into bedspreads. The quilting has a rich, textured appearance and is more crease-resistant than the unquilted fabrics. Because it is already lined with cotton lining, it is ready to be used for throw-over covers.

The simplest finish is to turn under a 3 cm (1¼ in) hem and stitch it all round for an instant bedcover. A contrasting flat border, rolled edge or frill would, however, give it a rather more professional finish.

Flat-border finish

MEASURING

Measure as before *(Fig. 33a, p. 45)*, and add a 1.5 cm (⅝ in) seam allowance all round.

If you are adding a flat border to a bedspread with square corners, the contrast border strips may be cut along the straight grain of the fabric. You will have to cut enough 8 cm (3¼ in) wide strips to make up the required length of border (for two sides and the bottom end; the top end does not need to have a border as a finish).

If the bedspread has rounded corners, you need to cut a continuous length of border on the bias *(p. 65)*, again about 8 cm (3¼ in) wide, to the length of the two sides plus the length of the bottom end.

REQUIREMENTS

Quilted fabric: See *Hint* on page 45.
Fabric for a flat-border finish

METHOD FOR SQUARE CORNERS

1. *Repeat step 1 on page 43.*

2. *With right side of border strip facing wrong side of quilting and raw edges together, sew border to quilting (first to the two sides)* (Fig. 34a).

3. *Fold border to the right side, press seam flat, and press in a 1 cm (⅜ in) hem along the raw edges of the border strips. Top-stitch the borders to the quilting through all thicknesses* (Fig. 34b).

4. *Repeat the same process along the bottom and the top (optional) of the throw-over bedspread, and make neat corners (Fig. 34b) or mitre the corners* (p. 68).

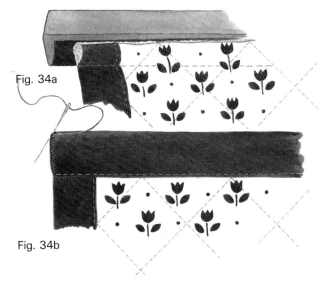

Fig. 34a

Fig. 34b

METHOD FOR ROUND CORNERS

1. *Cut out fabric and join width (see step 1 on page 43).*

2. *Fold over a double hem at the top of the quilting, and sew across.*

3. *Sew the bias strip, with its right side facing the wrong side of the quilting and raw edges together, to the quilting, starting at the top on one side. Stretch it slightly as you sew round the corners.*

4. *To finish, repeat step 3 for square corners* (Fig. 35).

Fig. 35

Rolled edge finish

MEASURING

Measure as before *(Fig. 33a, p. 45)*, and add a 1.5 cm (⅝ in) seam allowance all round. Adjust your measurements if you do not want the roll to trail on the floor.

REQUIREMENTS

Quilted fabric
Fabric for the roll: For a finished roll of 5 cm (2 in) diameter you will need a continuous length of bias binding *(p. 65)* to the length of sides plus the length of the bottom end, and 18 cm (7 in) wide.
Wadding (Batting): strip as long as bias, 16 cm (6 ¼ in) wide.

METHOD

1. *Cut out fabric and join widths (see step 1 on page 43).*
2. *Fold over a double hem at the top end of the quilting, and sew across, leaving 1.5 cm (⅝ in) open on each side.*
3. *With right sides and raw edges together, position the fabric strip over the quilting, and position the wadding (batting) on top of that. Leave 1.5 cm (⅝ in) of fabric sticking out over the two corners at the top (Fig. 36a).*

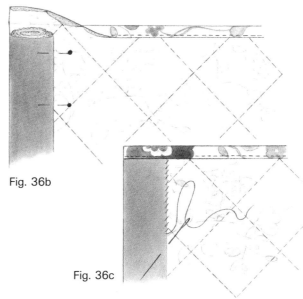

Fig. 36b

Fig. 36c

6. *Press 1.5 cm (⅝ in) hem on all remaining raw edges of bias strip, and fold over roll of wadding (batting). Slip-stitch in place all round (Fig. 36c) on previous stitching line.*

Fig. 36a

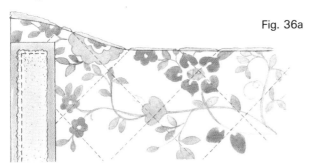

4. *Sew a 1.5 cm (⅝ in) seam through all thicknesses round the three sides (Fig 36a).*
5. *Roll wadding (batting) into a roll towards wrong side; pin into position round the three sides (Fig. 36b).*

ABOVE: A neat rounded corner on a quilted bedspread with a flat border and piping.

Piped finish with a frill

REQUIREMENTS

Quilting fabric

Piping: to go round 3 sides

Fabric for a frill: 2¼ × measurement round 3 sides
(p. 37); 10 cm (4 in) strips for a single frill and 18 cm
(7 in) strips for a double frill.

Bias binding: to go round 3 sides

METHOD

1. *Repeat step 1 on page 43.*

2. *Attach piping and frill to the three sides, following steps
3–6 on page 44.*

3. *Sew bias binding over the raw edges of the frill and
quilting* (Fig. 37a).

4. *Fold remaining raw edges at the top over twice, and sew
down this hem* (Fig. 37b).

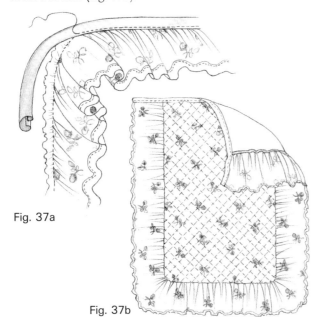

Fig. 37a

Fig. 37b

PATCHWORK QUILTS

A patchwork quilt must be one of the most rewarding home
sewing projects a person can tackle . . . and finish! It certainly
is a labour of love requiring care, dedication and patience.
Cotton fabrics are extremely suitable for use in patchwork. A
medium-weight cotton is easy to handle and a pleasure to sew,
the colours are well co-ordinated, and the designs are varied
and plentiful. Check fabric is also pre-shrunk. There is a huge
range of patchwork patterns to choose from and it would be
impossible to describe the making of them all, so I have chosen
three popular designs.

General guidelines

❏ Use fabrics of the same weight for your whole patchwork
project.

❏ Plan the design of your quilt, to scale, on graph paper. You
can then work out how much of each of the different fabrics you
need to purchase. Always allow a little bit extra.

❏ Accurate cutting and straight sewing are the key to success-
ful patchwork.

❏ Keep to the same seam allowance throughout, for example,
5 mm (¼ in).

❏ Back-stitch the ends of seams to strengthen them.

❏ Press the patches as you make them, but note that once
patchwork bedspreads have been quilted and lined, they should
never be pressed.

❏ Always join patchwork in sections to form squares or rectan-
gles, which can then be joined by sewing long straight seams.
When joining long strips, turn the work around so that each
strip is sewn on in the opposite direction to the one before. This
prevents an accumulative 'dragging' to one side.

❏ A lot of people are put off by the thought of all the accurate
measuring involved in patchwork. Remember that borders can
be sewn round a central panel of patchwork to bring it to the cor-
rect finished size. Always measure the panel to be bordered
widthwise and lengthwise through the centre to determine the

length of the borders. Borders should be sewn on starting in the centre of the panel and working outwards.

❏ It is almost impossible to quilt a large bedspread on a domestic sewing machine. Two valuable hints are:

1. Quilt small, manageable sections to within 5 cm (2 in) of the edges, always working from the centre outwards. Join the sections, leaving the quilting free. Cut 'tongue and groove' sections where quilting overlaps, and oversew with large herring-bone stitches *(Fig. 38a)*.

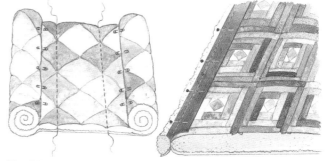

Fig. 38b

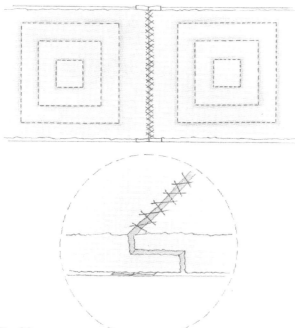

Fig. 38a

2. Place your patchwork over the quilting and pin in place. Roll up tightly from both ends towards the front and secure the rolls with safety pins *(Fig. 38b)*. Quilt in straight lines between the two rolls, starting in the centre and proceeding to unroll and quilt towards the sides *(Fig. 38b)*.

Fig. 39a

TO BIND AND LINE A QUILT

1. *The wadding (batting) used should extend over all four sides by about 3 cm (1 ¼ in) (fig. 39a).*

2. *Sew the binding to the right sides of the quilt through all thicknesses.*

3. *Place quilted patchwork on top of lining with wrong sides together, and pin and tack along sewing line (Fig. 39a).*

4. *Turn work over, and sew through all thicknesses just to the outside of the previous sewing line on the seam allowance (Fig. 39b).*

5. *Press in a 1 cm (⅜ in) hem on the binding, turn it over the wadding (batting) to the lining side, and hand-stitch it into place right round (Fig. 39c).*

6. *Bind the sides and then the top and the bottom. Neaten corners.*

Fig. 39b

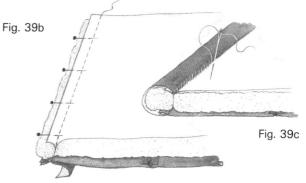

Fig. 39c

STANDARD QUILT SIZES
Single: 180 cm × 250 cm (70 in × 98 in)
Double: 250 cm × 250 cm (98 in × 98 in)
King: 280 cm × 270 cm (112 in × 108 in)

Pin-tuck and lace quilts

The two quilts that follow are variations of a basic pin-tuck and lace square.

The basic square

1. *Cut out squares of fabric 42 cm (16½ in).*
2. *Sew three 2 mm (⅛ in) pin-tucks (p. 67) vertically (Fig. 40a) and diagonally across centre of square.*
3. *Add lace and ribbon as shown (Fig. 40b).*

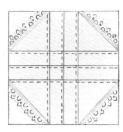
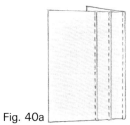
Fig. 40a   Fig. 40b

To make up a cream dream quilt

A plain cloth in white or cream is used for this quilt which is made up entirely of basic squares. Instructions for the basic square are given above.

CALCULATING HOW MANY BASIC SQUARES YOU WILL NEED

Size of bed	Number of squares
Single	4 × 6 = 24
Double	6 × 6 = 36
King	7 × 6 = 42

REQUIREMENTS
Fabric for basic squares and borders
Lace
Ribbon

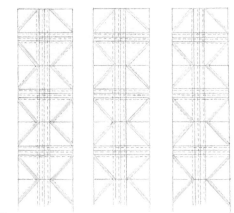
Fig. 41a

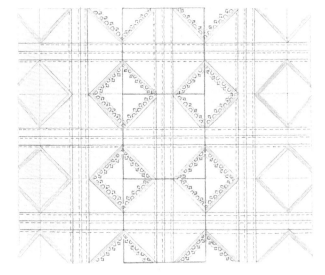
Fig. 41b

METHOD

1. *Make up the required number of basic squares.*
2. *Join squares* (Fig. 41a) *and make up quilt to required size with borders* (Fig. 41b).

To make a rose pin-tuck and lace quilt

Three different floral fabrics are used to make up this pretty quilt, one with a predominant rose motif. You can also experiment with your own choice of co-ordinating fabrics from any of the ranges now widely available.

CALCULATING HOW MANY BASIC SQUARES YOU WILL NEED

Size of bed	Number of squares
Single	$3 \times 4 = 12$
Double	$4 \times 4 = 16$
King	$5 \times 4 = 20$

REQUIREMENTS

Rose print fabric for basic squares: each 41 cm (16 in)
Lace
Ribbon
Rose motifs from rose print fabric: roughly 14 cm (5½ in) sq
Second floral fabric: rectangular pieces 39.5 cm × 4 cm (15½ × 1½ in)
Third floral fabric: rectangular pieces 39.5 cm × 8.5 cm (15½ × 3½ in)

METHOD

1. *Plan your quilt on graph paper. Make up required number of basic squares* (p. 50) *in rose print fabric.*
2. *Cut out required number of small squares (rose motifs from rose print fabric* [Fig. 42a]*).*
3. *Cut out required number of rectangular pieces of second and third floral fabrics* (Fig. 42b).
4. *Join the different components to required size* (Fig. 42c; Fig. 42d).

Fig. 42a

Fig. 42b

Fig. 42c

Fig. 42d

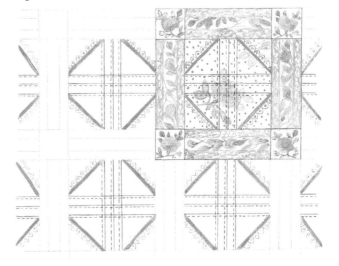

Log cabin quilt

If you can cut and sew straight, you can make this quilt. It consists of rectangular strips of fabric sewn round a central square, on top of a backing square of lining which strengthens the final product, gives it body, and serves as a guide to where to place the strips around the ever-increasing square.

The choice of fabric with regard to the colour and design is important. Traditionally, strips of light and dark background fabrics form opposite triangles on either side of the central square. Each square is made exactly the same. A bolder effect can be achieved if all the fabrics used have dark backgrounds and the only contrast is in the choice of colours, for example, pink and green, navy and maroon.

The most interesting result, as far as I am concerned, is achieved when a colour theme is decided upon, for example, maroon and navy, and strips of as many different fabrics as you can find in these two colours are used at random. In other words, although the squares are not all identical, they are similar as the navy strips always form the triangle on one side of the central square and the maroon strips on the other. (The central squares should always be identical.) This is a break from tradition, but the result is rich and stunning. The way the squares are placed creates different effects *(Fig. 43)*.

Most designs require equal rows of squares, widthwise and lengthwise. Strips are cut between 4 cm (1½ in) and 6 cm (2¼ in) wide, which includes a 5 mm (¼ in) seam allowance each side. The central square must be at least the same measurement as the width of the fabric strip, or bigger. I prefer cutting long strips of fabric, and then cutting and sewing each strip as needed. Accurate cutting of the strips, the central squares and the backing squares is the key to a good end product.

MEASURING

Measure as for bedspread *(p. 45)* or refer to standard sizes *(p. 50)*. Scale down measurements and transfer them to graph paper. Work out how many equal squares of between 15 cm

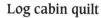
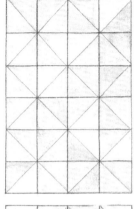

Fig. 43

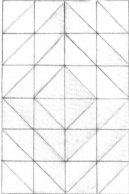
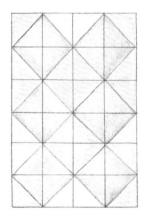

(6 in) and 30 cm (12 in) — size is optional — you will need widthwise and lengthwise. Take into account that the central panel of patchwork will be finished off with one or two borders round the sides. Once you have determined the size of your squares, work out what the size of the small central square will be as well as the number and width of the strips.

OPPOSITE: Dramatic and bold colours work well in a masculine bedroom. A log cabin quilt, a box-pleated valance and flat-bordered cushions give a tailored look to this room.

REQUIREMENTS
Cardboard template: the size of the square plus 5 mm (¼ in) seam allowance all round
Fabric: see instructions on measuring on page 52 (remember to allow for 5 mm [¼ in] seams)
Lining for backing squares: cut out using the template
Lining for the back of the quilt
Polyester wadding (batting)

METHOD FOR ONE SQUARE
1. *Find the centre of one backing square and position small central square on top of it (Fig. 44a).*
2. *With right sides together, position first fabric strip on top of central square. Sew and cut strip (Fig. 44b). Fold out strip, and press flat.*

Fig. 44a   Fig. 44b

Fig. 44c   Fig. 44d

3. *Repeat this process with the same strip of fabric, turning your square once anti-clockwise (Fig. 44c).*
4. *Repeat steps 2 and 3 with a contrasting strip of fabric (Fig. 44d).*
5. *Repeat steps 2–4 until square is the required size. Remember to press it.*

HINT *Do not stretch the fabric strips as you sew them.*

6. *When you have completed all your squares, trim them to the size of your cardboard template.*
7. *To assemble, spread your design out on the floor. Sew the squares together to make long strips, and then join the strips together.*
8. *Sew the borders round the sides of the central panel of the patchwork to make up the bedspread to your finished size (p. 50).*
9. *To quilt and line, see page 49.*

ABOVE: Elegant piped and flat-bordered scatter cushions on a log cabin quilt in maroon and navy.

FOUR-POSTER BEDS

Historically, a grand bed arrangement with formal bed curtains and valances, suspended from an ornate four-poster frame, reflected the status and style of the very wealthy. A more humble version of this style was also in common use for practical reasons like warmth and privacy. Today, the use of bed curtains, valances and canopies is purely decorative, a nostalgic reflection of a more romantic era.

The three components that make up the dressing of a four-poster bed are mock curtains, a valance and a canopy. They can all be used together, individually, or in combination. Because the valance and curtains can be seen from both sides, it is important that the lining is attractive (usually this will be a contrast fabric). The canopy that forms the roof over the bed has the right side of the fabric facing the bed, and ordinary lining can be used on top as this part is not visible.

The type of frame dictates the way the fabric is to be suspended from it. The methods described here will, hopefully, be applicable to most styles of four-poster bed.

Fig. 45a

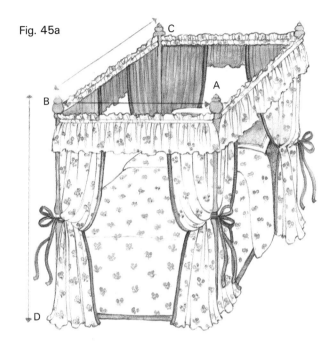

Mock curtains and valance for a brass and iron four-poster bed

> **NOTE** *The method that follows assumes that the bed has a top frame of iron rods that can be removed to be pushed through casings on the fabric.*

MEASURING

Measure the length of the short (A–B) and long (B–C) rods that form the top frame *(Fig. 45)*.

Measure the length (C–D) from the rod to the floor *(Fig. 45)*. The finished length of the valance will be 35 cm (14 in).

> **NOTE** *It is important that the length of the valance is in relation to the height of the bed.*

REQUIREMENTS

Fabric for the outside of curtains: add 8 cm (3¼ in) to rod-to-floor (B–D) measurement and cut 8 drops
Contrast fabric for inside of curtains: see above
Fabric for outside of valance: see box
Contrast fabric for the inside of the valance: see box
Fabric for frills: optional

> **CALCULATING FABRIC REQUIRED FOR A 35 CM (14 IN) VALANCE** *For outside, multiply length of long rod by two and divide by 150 cm (60 in) – standard fabric width – for number of drops for long side; repeat procedure with short rod. Multiply total number of drops by 47 cm (18½ in) to determine the amount of fabric required. For contrast fabric, multiply the total number of drops by 30 cm (12 in).*

ADDING A FRILL

If you want to add frills, apply them to the bottom edge of the valances and down the insides of all the curtains. Determine the total length of frill needed and use the formula on page 19 for double frills to work out the amount of fabric required.

METHOD FOR CURTAINS AND VALANCE

1. *Use two full drops of fabric and of contrast fabric to make two curtains for one side (if you find there is too much fabric, cut the drops down to a minimum width of 115 cm (45 in); the off-cuts can be used for frills).*

2. *With right sides and raw edges of fabric and contrast fabric together, sew a 1.5 cm (⅝ in) seam along both sides (frills must be sewn into inside seams at this point). Turn right side out, and press (Fig. 46a).*

3. *Turn under a small hem and then a 5 cm (2 in) hem at the bottom raw edge, and sew it in place (Fig. 46a).*

Fig. 46a

4. *With right sides and raw edges of fabric and contrast fabric for valance together, sew a 1.5 cm (⅝ in) seam round the two sides and the bottom edge (Fig. 46b). (Frills must be attached at this point.) Turn right side out, and press.*

Fig. 46b

5. *Press in a 2.5 cm (1 in) hem on the raw edge of the fabric that extends at the top, and press in a second fold, 9 cm (3½ in) from the edge of the hem (Fig. 46c).*

6. *Measure and mark off a line across width on contrast fabric, 26 cm (10¼ in) from bottom edge (Fig. 46c).*

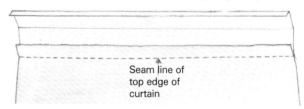

Seam line of top edge of curtain

Fig. 46c

7. *Position the seam line of the top edge of the curtains on this line with the contrast fabric facing up. (The two curtains are positioned to the sides of the valance.) Pin in place (Fig. 46c).*

8. *Flap the extended fabric at the back over at the fold line so that its edge meets the marked off line. Pin in position, and sew close to the edge through all thicknesses (Fig. 46c).*

9. *Sew another row of stitching 4 cm (1½ in) from this line to form the casing (adapt size of casing if necessary). The fabric above the casing forms a frill at the top of the valance when it is ruched over the rod (Fig. 46d).*

10. *Repeat this process to make valance and curtains for other three sides.*

11. *Hang the curtains and the valances by ruching them onto the iron rods (Fig. 46d). Tie the two curtains at each corner to the bed posts with attractive ribbons, braids or tie-backs.*

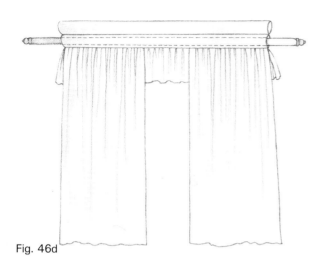

Fig. 46d

Wooden four-posters

The method described on page 56 can be adapted in the following manner to be used on a solid four-poster bed frame:

❏ Instead of making a casing *(step 9; p. 56)*, sew narrow curtain tape to the inside on the marked line. Small screw eyes are now all fixed along the outside of the top wooden frame, and the curtain hooks on the gathered curtain tape are hooked through these *(Fig. 47)*.

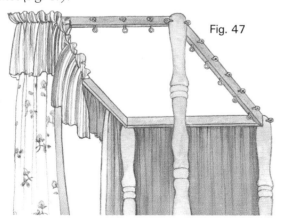

Fig. 47

❏ A canopy forming a roof over the bed can be added using the following method:

1. *For a flat canopy, cut a rectangle of fabric to the width and length measurement of the top frame with a 2 cm (¾ in) hem allowance all round.*

2. *Sew a 2 cm (¾ in) hem all around the canopy, and sew narrow curtain tape on top of it, along four sides.*

3. *Apply curtain hooks to the tape at regular intervals. Fix screw eyes round the bottom edge of the frame to correspond with the hooks on the canopy and hook the canopy on* (Fig. 47).

4. *For a ruched canopy, the length of the canopy is 1½ times the length of the frame. Gather the fullness by pulling in the curtain tape and hook to the screw eyes.*

❏ A valance can be sewn directly onto a canopy, which then simply lies on top of the frame with the valances hanging down the sides, holding it in position *(Fig. 48)*. Top-stitch a lining to the top to cover raw edges and seams.

Fig. 48

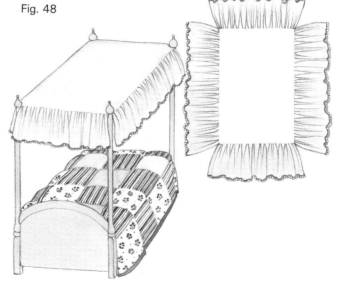

❏ Alternative to gathered valances are:

1. Straight valances can be scooped into casual swags by means of ties (see photograph on page 34).

2. A gathered valance can be made into a festoon valance by sewing narrow curtain tape to the inside at regular intervals and ruching it up *(Fig. 49)*. (Frills at the bottom will round this style off prettily.)

3. Fabric can be loosely draped over the frame (see illustration on page 7).

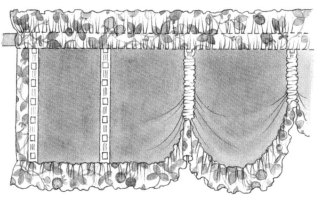

Fig. 49

Mock four-poster

If you would love to surround yourself with fabric and do not have a four-poster bed, you can simulate the effect easily and relatively inexpensively over your ordinary bed. Here are a few suggestions:

❏ A wooden frame, made to the measurement of the width and length of the bed, is suspended from the ceiling over the bed by means of ropes (attached to each corner of the frame), which are hung from screw eyes fixed to the ceiling (see photograph on page 34). Any of the canopies and valances mentioned before can be draped over this frame.

❏ A projecting pole installed centrally over the bed, either at the top or at the side, with fabric slung over it in an inverted

V-shape is an easy way to achieve a rather dramatic effect (see photograph on opposite page). The fabric is visible from both sides and should therefore be lined with a contrast fabric. The fabric is tied back to the corners of the bed.

❏ Two brass or wooden poles as long as the width of the bed are mounted to or suspended from the ceiling and fabric is draped over them. The fabric will hang behind the bed, fall into a soft swag over the bed, and hang midway down or right down to the end of the bed *(Fig. 50)*.

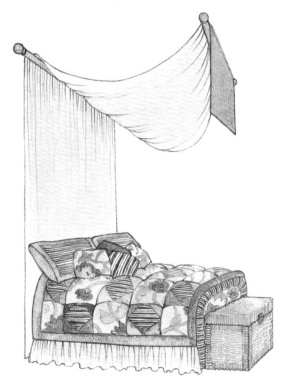

Fig. 50

OPPOSITE: Fabric ruched onto a pole over the centre of the bed and tied back to the corners lends an old-world charm to this sunny bedroom in candy pink, mint green and buttercup yellow.

Corona drapes

A corona can be made from a semi-circular piece of chipboard, attached to the wall by means of angle brackets. The curtains and valance of the corona are permanently fixed to the chipboard. First make and attach the piece of chipboard *(Fig. 51a)*, then add the curtains and valance.

Wooden fixture

REQUIREMENTS
A semi-circle of chipboard cut to a pattern
Two angle brackets
Two pieces of contrast fabric: cut to size of chipboard plus a 3 cm (1¼ in) seam allowance all round (fabric for top of wood optional)
Screw eyes: about 35
Narrow curtain tape to go round the circular front
A staple gun or tacks

METHOD FOR MAKING WOODEN FIXTURE
1. *Attach the angle brackets to the wood at the back, 10 cm (4 in) in from the sides* (Fig. 51a).
2. *Position the fabric on top of the wood (optional), fold over the excess, and staple it down. Do the same at the bottom (over the angle brackets).*
3. *Attach the screw eyes right round the bottom, close to the edge, spacing them 5 cm (2 in) apart* (Fig. 51a).
4. *Staple curtain tape round the circular front* (Fig. 51a).
5. *Attach the wooden fixture to the wall, about 150 cm (60 in) above the bed.*

Curtains and valance

MEASURING
Measure the length for the curtains from the centre of the wooden fixture in front to the floor *(Fig. 51b)*, and add 10 cm (4 in). The length of the valance is optional — about 30 cm to 40 cm (12 in to 16 in) plus 5 cm (2 in) all round.

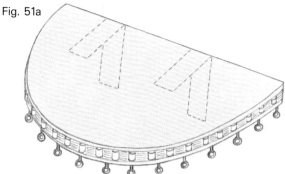

Fig. 51a

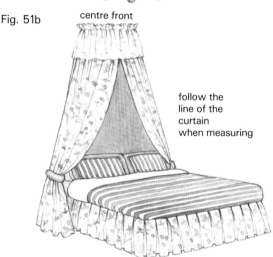

Fig. 51b

centre front

follow the line of the curtain when measuring

REQUIREMENTS
Fabric for outside curtains: cut 2 drops to required length
Contrast fabric for inside curtains: as above
Fabric for frills down the inside of curtains: optional
Narrow curtain tape and hooks for curtains
Fabric for outside valance: cut 2 drops of fabric to the required length
Contrast fabric for inside valance: see above
Fabric for frills for bottom of valance: optional
Pencil pleat curtain tape and hooks

METHOD FOR MAKING CURTAINS AND VALANCE

1. *For the curtains, join the widths of the fabric for the outside, and do the same with the contrast fabric for the inside.*

2. *With right sides and raw edges together, join the fabric and contrast fabric along the two sides and across the top. (Optional frills can be sewn into the two side seams at this stage.)*

3. *Turn right side out, and press all seams.*

4. *Sew narrow curtain tape onto the fabric (outside) 2 cm (¾ in) away from the top edge. Gather curtain tape and attach hooks 5 cm (2 in) apart. (The gathers can be spaced so that more fullness hangs round the circular front than across the straight back.)*

5. *At this point, hook the curtains onto the screw eyes on the wooden fixture. Determine the position of the slits through which the tie-backs will hold the curtains to the side of the bed (Fig. 51c). Hold the curtain in this position, and adjust the hemline by cutting away the extra length towards the back but leaving enough fabric to turn in the hems (Fig. 51d).*

6. *Take the curtains down again. Press and sew in a 6 cm (2¼ in) hem on fabric and contrast fabric.*

7. *Make 10 cm (4 in) long slits at marked positions on fabric and contrast fabric (Fig. 51c).*

8. *Make tie-backs out of the off-cut pieces of fabric.*

9. *To make the valance, join the widths of the fabric, and do the same with the contrast fabric. With right sides and raw edges together, join the two pieces, allowing 2 cm (¾ in) for seams all round, and allowing an opening for turning right side out. Clip corners, and turn right side out, slip-stitch opening closed, and press seams.*

10. *Sew pencil pleat tape to the top of the valance on the contrast fabric (inside). Gather up, and attach hooks.*

11. *Hook the curtains to the screw eyes, and the valance to the curtain tape on the wooden fixture (Fig. 51e).*

12. *Slip the tie-backs through the slits, and hook them to cuphooks attached to the wall on either side of the bed (as in Fig. 51b).*

Fig. 51e

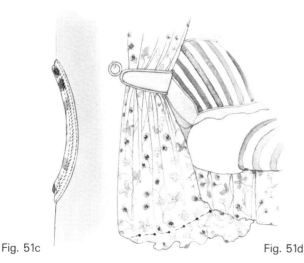

Fig. 51c

Fig. 51d

TABLE-CLOTHS

Round tables, covered with floor-length table-cloths and round or square over-cloths, complete the look in a feminine bedroom. These covered tables are practical in that they usually hold bedside lamps, books and magazines.

A single, larger round table draped with a lovely cloth and bearing a lamp, a plant or a bowl of flowers, some beautifully framed photographs and other decorative personal paraphernalia can create a focal point in a room.

> **HINT** *For an instant drape table, rest a circle of chipboard on any solid base and cover it with a floor-length round table-cloth.*

A round table-cloth

MEASURING

Measure the diameter (A–B) of the top of the table as well as the length to the floor (B–C) *(Fig. 52a)*. The diameter of the table-cloth is the diameter of the table (A–B) plus twice the length (B–C). Make a pattern *(p. 11)*.

REQUIREMENTS

For a 150 cm (60 in) wide fabric:

Diameter of table-cloth	Fabric without pattern repeat	Fabric with 32–63 cm (12½–25 in) pattern repeat
150 cm (60 in)	1.55 m (62 in)	1.55 m (62 in)
180 cm (70 in)	2.95 m (3¼ yd)	3.3 m–3.6 m (3½ yd–4 yd)
200 cm (80 in)	3.4 m (3⅞ yd)	4 m (4⅜ yd)
250 cm (100 in)	4.6 m (5 yd)	5.2 m (5¾ yd)

METHOD

1. *For the centre panel of the table-cloth, cut off a piece of fabric equal to the finished diameter plus a 2 cm (¾ in) hem allowance. Mark the centre along the width.*

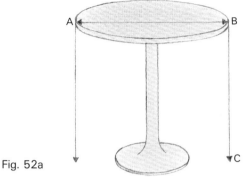

Fig. 52a

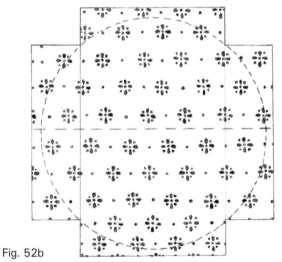

Fig. 52b

2. *Cut remaining fabric in half, lengthwise, mark centres along width, and join a piece to each side of centre panel, lining up centre marks (Fig. 52b). Press seams flat.*
3. *Make a quarter-circle pattern by drawing an arc equal to the radius (diameter ÷ 2), fold the piece of fabric into four, and place pattern on fabric (Fig. 52c, p. 63).*
4. *Cut around pattern through all thicknesses.*
5. *Fold and press in a 1 cm (⅜ in) double hem. Stitch. Alternatively, sew bias binding to the raw edge (p. 66).*

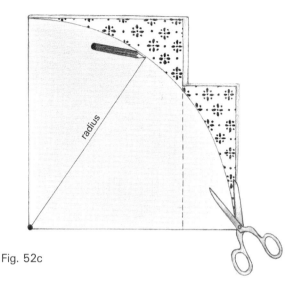

Fig. 52c

ADDING A FRILL TO THE BOTTOM

Decide on the width of the frill, and deduct this measurement all round from the diameter of the finished cloth. Multiply this measurement by 22 and divide the answer by 7 to determine the circumference. Use the formula on page 69 to work out how much fabric you need for the frill. Join the frill to the table-cloth, following the instructions on pages 17–18.

Over-cloths

A smaller round or square over-cloth in a contrast fabric looks lovely over a floor-length round table-cloth.

❑ The raw edge of the over-cloth may be finished with bias binding in matching or contrasting fabric.

❑ Ruche a frilled round or square over-cloth by means of narrow curtain tape *(Fig. 49, p. 58)*, and sew fabric bows above the gathers.

❑ Sew pin-tucks along the edges of a square over-cloth, over-lapping them at the corners *(p. 67)*.

❑ A contrast border with neatly mitred corners *(p. 68)* finishes off a square over-cloth beautifully.

TOP: The double frill as well as the gathered skirt of this kidney-shaped dressing table have been sewn onto a fitted top.

ABOVE: A deep gathered frill finishes the edge of a round table-cloth.

Fitted table-cloths

A fitted table-cloth has a flat piece of fabric covering the top of the table with a gathered skirt attached to it. This type of table-cloth can be used on round, square, rectangular and kidney-shaped tables.

MEASURING

Make a paper pattern to the size and shape of the table top with a 1.5 cm (⅝ in) seam allowance all round.

REQUIREMENTS

Fabric for the top: enough to cut out 1 pattern
Piping: enough to go round the pattern
Fabric for the skirt or frill: Measure right round the pattern, or in the case of a round table, work out the circumference *(p. 62)*. Use the formula on page 62 to determine the amount of fabric needed.

METHOD

1. *Cut the fabric for the top of the table-cloth according to the pattern.*
2. *With right sides and raw edges together, pin and tack piping to the top.*
3. *Join the pieces of fabric for the frill. Gather and join to the top according to instructions on pages 17–18.*

COVERING A SHAPED DRESSING TABLE

These kidney-shaped dressing tables have an old-world charm of frivolity and self-indulgence. Plain uncovered dressing tables are available and can be covered in a variety of styles. These covers are easy enough to make yourself. The method described here is illustrated in Figure 53.

❑ Use the method described for a fitted table-cloth with a gathered skirt *(above)*, using a paper pattern of the kidney-shaped top, for loose cover. Remember to leave an opening in the centre front for access to the open shelves.

❑ Gather a short, contrasting valance together with the skirt before sewing it to the top. The valance has no split in the centre front, although the skirt does.

❑ Add trimmings of your choice, for example, cotton lace, frills *(p. 19)*, prairie points *(p. 67)*, or bind all raw edges with a contrast fabric *(p. 66)*.

❑ Horizontal rows of pin-tucks *(p. 67)*, lace and ribbon can be sewn to the skirt across the width before gathering it up.

❑ A curtain track can be bent and mounted to follow the shape round the edge of the table top. Alternatively, small screw eyes can be attached round the edge, or narrow curtain tape stapled right round. In all these cases, a skirt is gathered on narrow curtain tape, and hooked through either the runners, screw eyes or tape pockets. A loose cover with a frill attached is fitted over the top of the table, concealing the 'mechanics' underneath.

Fig. 53

SEWING TECHNIQUES

The basic sewing techniques are described here. Your machine may have attachments that enable it to master these techniques more easily.

Bias binding

Bias binding is used to finish raw edges and to add a decorative finishing touch to many soft furnishing items. It is also used to cover piping cord to trim seams neatly. Because it is cut on the bias, that is, against the straight grain of the fabric, it has some stretch, and this makes it easy to use round curves and corners.

METHOD 1

1. *Find the diagonal line of a rectangular piece of fabric by folding over a corner at 45 degrees (Fig. 54a).*
2. *Mark fold line, and continue marking diagonal lines parallel to fold line, to required width of binding (Fig. 54b).*
3. *Cut out the strips, and join them at right angles, right sides together. Press seams, and trim corners. (Fig. 54c).*

METHOD 2 (CONTINUOUS STRIP OF BINDING)

1. *Take a rectangle of fabric that is at least twice as long as it is wide.*
2. *Fold over a corner at 45 degrees to mark the diagonal grain of the fabric. Cut out the triangle, and add it to the opposite side with straight sides together, so that the slanting lines are parallel (Fig. 55a).*
3. *Mark diagonal lines at equal distances parallel to the slanting line, starting on one side. Cut off the last piece if not equal to the bias width.*
4. *Draw a 5 mm (¼ in) seam line on each straight side. Mark points A, B, C, D, E and F (Fig. 55a).*

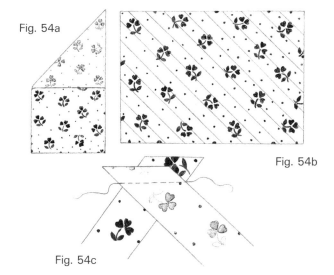

Fig. 54a

Fig. 54b

Fig. 54c

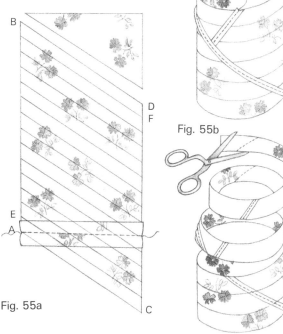

Fig. 55a

Fig. 55b

Fig. 55c

5. *With right sides together, form a tube by pinning points C to E and F to B, and pinning the seam in between along the marked seam line, thus joining side C–D to side E–B (Fig. 55b). The marked off diagonal lines must meet exactly. Sew along the seam line, and press the seam flat.*
6. *Start cutting at one end on the marked line, and continue cutting until you have one long strip* (Fig. 55c).

Piping

You can make your own piping by wrapping bias binding around piping cord and encasing it by sewing close to the piping cord with a zip foot attached to your machine *(Fig. 56a)*. Join piping cord by butting two ends and tying thread around tightly *(Fig. 56b)*. Make the binding wide enough to allow for a 5 mm (¼ in) seam allowance on the piping. When sewing piping into the seam of an article, use your zip foot attachment and sew as close to the cord as possible.

To join two pieces of piping: unpick a bit of the stitching on one end, trim about 1 cm (⅜ in) of the cord away, and fold the bias fabric over to the inside *(Fig. 56c)*. Push the other end inside and encase it by stitching down the folded bias *(Fig. 56d)*.

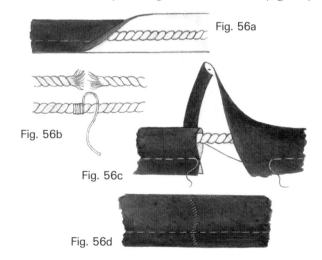

Fig. 56a

Fig. 56b

Fig. 56c

Fig. 56d

Binding an edge

❏ Fold ready-made binding over a raw edge, and carefully sew through all thicknesses *(Fig. 57)*.
❏ Position right sides and raw edges of binding and fabric together. Sew together, making a seam as wide as your machine foot *(Fig. 58a)*. Fold the binding to the wrong side of the fabric, and slip-stitch it in place close to the previous stitching line *(Fig. 58b)*.
❏ Position right side of binding to wrong side of fabric, and sew together, making a seam as wide as your machine foot. Fold binding to the right side, and top-stitch as close to the edge of the binding as possible *(Fig. 59)*.

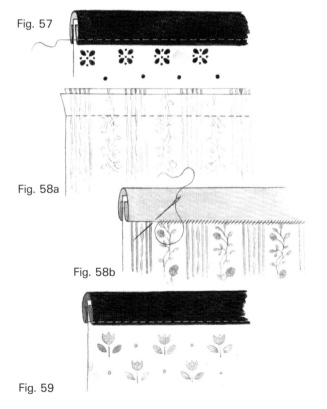

Fig. 57

Fig. 58a

Fig. 58b

Fig. 59

Pin-tucks

Pin-tucks add a decorative touch to many soft furnishing items. They can be made to overlap on corners, and form a beautiful trimming on square cushions or table-cloths. They can vary in size from a few millimetres to about 1 cm (⅜ in).

Allow extra fabric according to the size and number of pin-tucks, mark their position at regular intervals, and press in the folds. Sew equal distances away from the folds to form rows of pin-tucks. Press the pin-tucks to face in the same direction *(Fig. 60)*.

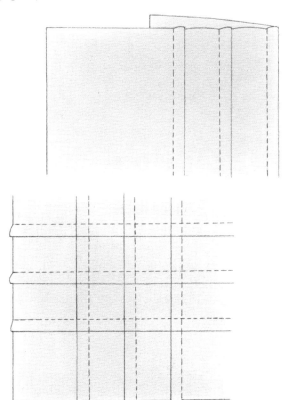

Fig. 60

Fig. 61a

Fig. 61b

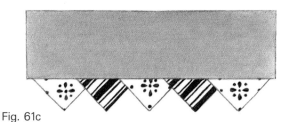

Fig. 61c

Prairie points

This edging gives an elegant, tailored finish, and is quite easy to make. You will need enough squares in different colours and designs to make up the length required (divide the length required by the diagonal measurement of the finished square to work out how many squares you need).

METHOD
1. *Fold a piece of square material twice to make a smaller square* (Fig. 61a).
2. *Line up the folded squares so that they overlap slightly, and stitch through the centre* (Fig. 61b).
3. *Position right side of fabric over strip of squares and sew just under previous stitching line on strip. Fold right side of fabric up, and press flat* (Fig. 61c).

Mitred corners

FOR A BORDER THAT IS SEWN ON TOP OF AN ARTICLE

1. *With right sides and raw edges together, stitch border to fabric, stopping a few centimetres away from the corners (Fig. 62a).*

2. *Overlap the borders, and mark the corners (Fig. 62b). With right sides together, join borders along marked lines, leaving a small hem allowance on the inside (Fig. 62b).*

3. *Trim seam, and complete stitching lines to corner.*

4. *Turn border to the right side, press seam, and press in the small hem. Top-stitch close to the edge of the border through all thicknesses (Fig. 62c).*

FOR A BORDER THAT IS ADDED ON TO AN ARTICLE

1. *Repeat step 1 opposite.*

2. *Overlap the borders, and mark the corner as shown (Fig. 63a). With right sides together, join borders along marked line, stopping a few millimetres away from the inside (Fig. 63b).*

3. *Trim seam, and complete stitching lines to corner. Fold away from article, and press (Fig. 63c).*

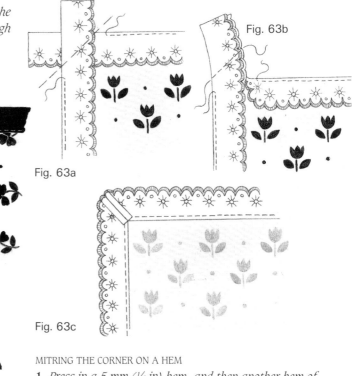

Fig. 63b

Fig. 63a

Fig. 63c

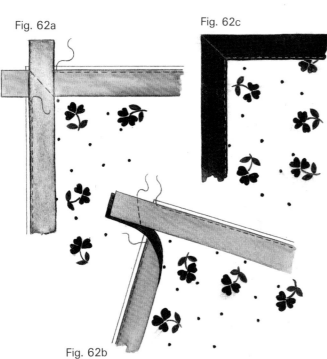

Fig. 62a

Fig. 62c

Fig. 62b

MITRING THE CORNER ON A HEM

1. *Press in a 5 mm (¼ in) hem, and then another hem of the required width. Open out.*

2. *Fold each corner to the inside to meet the intersection of the inner fold lines, and press in diagonal fold line (Fig. 64a). Open out.*

3. *With right sides together, fold two halves of diagonal line onto each other, and stitch along this line (Fig. 64b). Do the same with remaining corners, trim seams, and press open.*
4. *Turn these seams over to the inside, and press along fold lines between corners (Fig. 64c).*

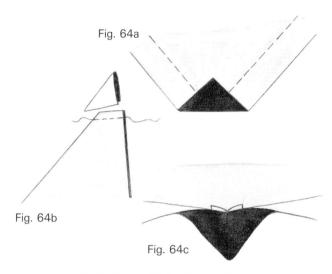

Fig. 64a

Fig. 64b

Fig. 64c

Calculating widths for gathering

Determine the total fabric width to be gathered by measuring the area on which the gathers must be sewn (for example, the measurement around the four sides of a double-bed valance = 517 cm [207 in]). Multiply this measurement by the required fullness (for example, 517 cm [207 in] × 2 = 1 034 cm [414 in]). Divide the answer by the width of the fabric (for example, 150 cm [60 in]) to determine the number of fabric widths to be cut and joined to make up the ungathered length (for example, 1 034 cm ÷ 150 [414 in ÷ 60 in] = 6.89). Round off the answer to the nearest whole number (for example, 7). Multiply the number of fabric widths by the finished depth of the frill plus hem and seam allowances (for example, 7 × 43 cm = 3 m [7 × 17 in = 3 yd]) to determine the amount of fabric required.

Allowing for a pattern repeat

Measure the distance between two repeating designs, for example, 32 cm (12½ in). Divide the finished depth of the frill plus hem and seam allowances by the pattern repeat and round off the answer to the next whole number (for example, the measurement for a double-bed valance: 43 cm ÷ 32 [17¼ ÷ 12½ in] = 1.34 [2]). Multiply this figure by the pattern repeat to determine new cut length (for example, 2 × 32 cm [12½ in] = 64 cm [25 in]). Multiply the new cut length by the number of widths required to determine the amount of fabric required (for example, 7 × 64 cm [25 in] = 4.48 m [4 ft 6 in]).

ABOVE: Prairie points decorate the top and bottom of this shaped dressing table for an interesting finish.

USEFUL ADDRESSES

Most of the supplies required for the cushion and cover projects are available at local fabric or textile stores (particularly those carrying upholstery fabrics) or quilting shops. Many discount department stores also carry appropriate fabrics, foam pieces, and polyester batting and fiberfill in the fabric or craft supply department. To acquire some of the fillings such as shredded foam, styrofoam pellets, kapok, and feathers and down, you may need to find an upholstery fabric and supply shop. Check your area Yellow Pages listings for: Upholstery Supplies; Foam Rubber; and Cushions. To locate fabric stores, check Yellow Pages listings under: Fabric Shops; Upholstery Supplies; Draperies and Curtains; Craft Supplies; and Quilting Materials and Supplies.

There are numerous mail order suppliers of fabric and upholstery supplies. Following is a partial listing of major suppliers who offer catalogs or can tell you who distributes their product in your area.

Fabric Suppliers
Many of these suppliers carry cotton fabrics, which are recommended for most of the patterns in this book
.
Alexandra's Homespun Textiles
A Division of The Seraph
5606 East Rt. 37
Delaware, OH 43015
614-369-1817
Manufacturer and mail order retailer of authentic homespun reproduction textiles. Carries over 40 patterns and has access to over 2,000 upholstery fabrics. Send $6.00 for color catalog.

Laura Ashley
1300 MacArthur Blvd.
Mahwah, NJ 07430
800-223-6917
Manufacturer of decorating fabrics with retail outlets. Call for name of store or distributor nearest you.

Britex Fabrics
146 Geary St.
San Francisco, CA 94108
415-392-2910
Retail store offering over 7,000 different fabrics. Personalized swatch service available upon request. Send $5.00 for fabric samples—specify your project, desired colors, type of fibers, quantity needed, style of decorating, and any price considerations. Keep in mind that large-scale patterns are difficult to swatch.

Homespun Fabrics and Draperies
P.O. Box 3223-SC
Ventura, CA 93006
805-642-8111
Mail order company offering 100% cotton fabrics in seamless 10-foot widths. Also carries sheers and linings. Send $2.00 for a catalog and swatches.

International Fabric Collection
3445 West Lake Rd.
Erie, PA 16505
800-462-3891 or
814-838-0740
FAX 814-838-9057
Mail order company with an assortment of specialty cottons from India, Liberty of London prints, African prints from Senegal, American cottons, and Japanese prints, among others. Send $3.00 for catalog.

Norton House
P.O. Box 579
Wilmington, VT 05363
802-464-7213
Sells a selection of 100% cotton fabrics for quilting and home decorating. Send $2.00 for catalog.

Waverly Fabrics.
800-423-5881
Manufacturer of drapery and upholstery fabrics. Call for name of a distributor near you.

Additional Supplies

Buffalo Batt & Felt Corp.
3307 Walden Ave.
Depew, NY 14043
716-683-4100
Mail order company carrying polyester fiberfill, batting, and pillow inserts in various sizes. Send $1.00 for price list and samples.

Lace Heaven Inc.
2524 Dauphin Island Parkway
Mobile, AL 36605
205-478-5644
Mail order company offering large selection of laces of all types. Send $3.00 for illustrated catalog.

BIBLIOGRAPHY

N & M Zips Co.
P.O. Box 1200
So. Norfolk, CT 06856
203-866-1540
Carries custom-made aluminum or plastic zippers in a variety of sizes, colors, and styles. Call or write for order form.

National Thread and Supply
695 Red Oak Road
Stockbridge, GA 30281
800-847-1001
Mail order company offering general sewing supplies, including zippers for upholstery, Velcro fasteners, chalks, pins, linings, seam binding, scissors, drapery supplies, piping cord, and miscellaneous speciality tools and supplies. Send for free catalog.

Newark Dressmaker Supply
6473 Ruch Road
(Dept. 850)
P.O. Box 20730
Lehigh Valley, PA 18002
215-837-7500
Mail order company carrying supplies for home sewers, craftspeople, and needlecrafters, including

fasteners and bindings, fabrics, interfacings, drapery and upholstery materials, measuring tools and much more. Send $1.00 for catalog.

S & B Sewing Notions
185 Gordon Rd.
Willowdale, ONT M2P 1E7
CANADA
416-445-3577
FAX 416-445-2682
Mail order and retail outlet offering sewing notions and supplies including books, cutting tools, lace, and more. Send $2.00 for catalog.

Sewing Emporium/Sew Easy Products
Gil Murray
1079 Third Avenue, #B
Chula Vista, CA 91910
619-420-3490
Mail order source for sewing accessories for making drapery, costumes, arts and crafts, embroidery, upholstery, or decorating. Send $4.95 for current catalog and handbook.

Many home and interior decorating magazines are excellent sources of additional ideas and supplier names and addresses. Following are a few suggestions of magazines you may find at your local library, grocery store, fabric store, or newsstand.

American HomeStyle
Better Homes & Gardens
Canadian House & Home
Colonial Homes
Country Living
Decorating (Better Homes and Gardens Special Interest Publications)

Family Circle
Good Housekeeping
Home Magazine
Interior Design
Ladies' Home Journal
Metropolitan Home
Town & Country
Women's Day

ABOVE: Bow cushions in rainbow pastels.

INDEX